TIA SHARP
A FAMILY BETRAYAL

NIGEL CAWTHORNE

TIA SHARP
A FAMILY BETRAYAL

JOHN BLAKE

Published by John Blake Publishing Ltd,
3 Bramber Court, 2 Bramber Road,
London W14 9PB, England

www.johnblakepublishing.co.uk

www.facebook.com/Johnblakepub facebook
twitter.com/johnblakepub twitter

This edition published in 2013

ISBN: 978 1 78219 223 7

British Library Cataloguing-in-Publication Data:

A catalogue record for this book is available from the British Library.

Design by www.envydesign.co.uk

Printed and bound in Great Britain by CPI Group (UK) Ltd

3 5 7 9 10 8 6 4 2

Papers used by John Blake Publishing are natural, recyclable products made
from wood grown in sustainable forests. The manufacturing processes conform
to the environmental regulations of the country of origin.

Every attempt has been made to contact the relevant copyright-holders,
but some were unobtainable. We would be grateful if the
appropriate people could contact us.

CONTENTS

INTRODUCTION

The death of a child is always extremely upsetting. The cold-blooded murder of a child is unbelievably hard to bear. The cold-blooded murder of a child by a stranger is one thing; the cold-blooded murder of a child by one of the family is quite another. And the murder of a child by a trusted member of the family with a sexual motivation is one of the worst crimes imaginable.

London was basking in the glory of the 2012 Olympic Games. The attention of the whole world was focused on the city. British athletes were climbing up the medal table and the whole nation was feeling pleased with itself. It was putting on a great show, and the Games, by their very nature, showed human beings aspiring to be the best they can be. But somewhere in an outer suburb, just 14 miles from the main stadium and less than 10 miles from Greenwich Park where the equestrian events were held, a dark heart was beating.

A 12-year-old girl with all the promise of her young life ahead of her had gone missing. Soon people were dreading the worst. We had been down this road before. Holly Wells and Jessica Chapman went missing in Soham in 2002. Thirteen-year-old Milly Dowler went missing on the way home from school also in 2002. Two-year-old James Bulger disappeared from a shopping centre in 1993. We still remember the victims of the Moors murderers in the 1960s – the body of one of them, Keith Bennett, is still missing. And the hunt for Madeleine McCann who disappeared in Portugal in 2007 still goes on.

There were other perplexing cases abroad. Eleven-year-old Jaycee Lee Dugard was kidnapped in California in 1991 and was held as a sex slave in paedophile Phillip Garrido's back garden for 18 years. Natascha Kampusch was abducted in Austria at the age of ten in 1998 and held for eight years. Gina DeJesus, who vanished at the age of 14, Amanda Berry, taken at 16, and Michelle Knight, kidnapped at 21, were allegedly held in the cellar of Ariel Castro in Cleveland, Ohio. They emerged in May 2013 after seemingly enduring the unendurable for between nine and ten years. Holly Wells, Jessica Chapman, Milly Dowler and James Bulger were all found dead. There is still some small hope that Madeleine McCann might be found alive – just as there was the day Tia Sharp went missing. In Tia's case, though, it was not to be.

Her plight tugged at the heartstrings of the nation. Hundreds quit watching the TV coverage of the Olympics to search for her or to hold candlelit vigils outside her house or at the bus stop where it was thought, at first, she had been abducted.

From the beginning, the police had their suspicions. These were soon shared by those who inhabit the Twittersphere and other social networks. The weekend the Olympics ended, Tia's body was found and her killer was arrested. He denied everything but few believed him.

At the very time Hazell was being arrested and charged, Mo Farah won his second gold medal and Usain Bolt his third. It seemed we were being shown the very best of what human beings can aspire to, and the very worst, side by side. While Farah, Bolt and, indeed, Tia seemed as if fallen straight from heaven, Hazell was a devil that had risen from the pits of hell.

The triumph of the Olympics was, at the opposite end of the spectrum, matched by the tragedy of Tia Sharp. As far as we know, she had no ambitions to be an athlete – although watching the Olympics might have inspired her, as it did so many other youngsters. Rather, she wanted to become an actress. But no ambition she may have had will ever be fulfilled now. She will not even be able to enjoy the more modest achievements of finishing her education, having a job, seeing something of the world and having a child and a family of her own.

The person who snuffed out all her possibilities was someone who had brought little good into this world. A violent and self-centred man, he had a long criminal record. Whether he should ever have been trusted with a young girl just reaching maturity is open to question. A devious man and an accomplished liar, Stuart Hazell managed to fool all of those around him.

When Tia went missing, the family rallied round. Those closest to him believed he was being wrongly accused by people that didn't know him. He went out searching for the child, made public appeals for her safe return and continued to deny that he had anything to do with her murder until the denial could be maintained no longer.

But who can point a finger at the family? Blame has been laid at the feet, for example, of Tia's real father, Steven. However, he did not abandon Tia – he was stopped from having any contact with her. Perhaps if he had been allowed access, none of this would have happened. However, any one of us can be fooled. Wouldn't we all like to believe the best of someone, rather than the worst? No one is going to advertise the fact that they have a sexual interest in young children. They are going to lie and cheat and dissemble. Because most of us have a good nature, we can all be taken in – and doesn't that mean that all of our children are in danger?

Nigel Cawthorne
Bloomsbury, May 2013
www.nigel-cawthorne.com

CHAPTER ONE

MISSING

Around midday on Friday, 3 August 2012, 12-year-old Tia Sharp had apparently vanished. It was then, the police said, that she had last been seen leaving her grandmother's house in New Addington, south London, where she had been staying for the weekend. It was the house in which she had spent much of her early life.

New Addington is a notoriously deprived area on the outskirts of Croydon. Begun in the 1930s and completed in the 1960s, it has a reputation for gang violence and anti-social behaviour, low educational standards, high unemployment and a high proportion of teenage mothers. A notorious 'Addo' gang took a prominent part in the 2011 London riots and 8 members were jailed for more than 25 years for around 100 offences.

The local shopping parade includes a takeaway, a betting shop and a supermarket selling discounted super-strength lagers and ciders. On the window of the local pub, the Randall Tavern, that day there was a police poster offering a reward for witnesses to an attempted murder in the neighbourhood.

It was said that 12-year-old Tia was allowed out on her own into this area. The story was that she was going to The Whitgift Centre in Croydon four miles away to buy some flip-flops before returning to her home in Mitcham, five miles further on, where Tia lived with her 31-year-old mother Natalie, her 27-year-old step-father David Niles, and her brothers, 3-year-old Jack and 1-year-old Harry.

'She has not been seen since,' said a spokesman. Her parents reported her missing at 6pm that same evening.

It was thought that she was carrying a small amount of cash – maybe £10 – but, curiously, she was not carrying her London Oyster transport card or her mobile phone. They had been left behind at her grandmother's house, number 20, The Lindens. Her description was given as 'white, slim, about 4ft 5in tall, and she usually wears glasses'. Tia's eyesight was poor. She was wearing a yellow bandeau-style boob tube over a white bra with visible cross straps, light grey leopard-skin leggings and black-and-pink Nike trainers. She had just turned 12 on 30 June and was a pupil at Raynes Park High School. The police appealed to anyone who had seen a girl answering her description in the Croydon, New Addington or Merton areas.

It was, the police added, 'out of character for Tia to go missing'. They were checking CCTV footage and liaising with other forces.

Although the reports in the Sunday newspapers were matter-of-fact, it was plain that there was cause for concern here. By the time the papers had gone to press, a young girl with no history of taking off hadn't been seen for 36 hours. Already some 200 neighbours had been out searching for her and Twitter was flooded with appeals.

Her aunt Jasmine Hart tweeted, 'It is unlikely that she ran away as it is completely out of character which is why this has become so serious.'

According to the *Sun*, former *Strictly Come Dancing* judge Arlene Phillips, ex-So Solid Crew member Lisa Maffia and glamour model Nicola McLean were among those supporting the search. By the following day, *Fifty Shades of Grey* author E.L. James, Jessie J and Coleen Nolan had joined the fray.

Jessie J tweeted, 'Croydon girl missing – please help find her'.

While singer, TV presenter and *Daily Mirror* columnist Coleen Nolan added, 'This girl is 12 and missing… please help find missing girl Tia Sharp'.

By then the police were saying that they believed she had been abducted within minutes of leaving her grandmother's house. They were searching a nearby wood, known as Birchwood, and were trying to trace a white van seen cruising the area around the time Tia disappeared.

But Tia's mum Natalie had said it was unlikely her daughter had been abducted. 'If anyone had tried to grab her, she would have fought like mad,' she told friends.

And Aunt Jasmine remained confident that Tia would be found safe. 'She's very smart and old enough to know how to get around, and was given money to buy shoes,' she said.

But Tia's step-father, 29-year-old David Niles, was distraught, saying, 'Our family is heartbroken. We are at our wits' end.' Screaming with emotion, he added, 'Just find my little girl!'

As Tia was not carrying her mobile phone, the police could not use triangulation between masts – a technique used by authorities to pin-point exactly where a mobile phone is by measuring the strength of the signal on three nearby telephone masts – to locate her or track the route she took. Though she did not have her travel card with her, it is possible to get on buses without one, and the police appealed to anyone who had seen her to get in touch.

Scotland Yard's serious-crime squad was brought in to help local officers who were scouring the hours of film footage taken from shops in The Whitgift Centre. They had already been through the footage from the shops around her grandmother's house in The Linden's area of New Addington and buses she may have taken – and had found nothing. Detectives were also combing the social-networking sites Tia used and checking phone and computer records to see who she had been in touch with.

The wood, just half a mile from the house, was still cordoned off. A hair bobble and a pair of glasses like Tia's had been found there but her mother Natalie said they were not hers. Some 8,000 leaflets were handed out and Tia's step-dad David, a builder who lived with her mother Natalie in nearby Mitcham, led the family's dealings with the press.

'Last time I saw her was on Thursday morning as I was going to work,' he said. 'She went to her nan's that day and

4

was going to come back on Monday. We are not good at the moment. I just want to thank everyone who has come out and been there to help us. I appreciate it so much. I love my kids to bits. Please keep on searching for my girl.'

The family, he said, were 'frantic with worry… It's unthinkable but you can't help fearing the worst.'

Tia's mother Natalie later recalled how Tia departed to stay with her grandmother Christine Bicknell at the house in New Addington she shared with window-cleaner Stuart Hazell. 'My phone pinged,' she said. 'It was a text message from Stuart. It said, "Tell Tia that she can stay the weekend with us. I've not got work tomorrow. Mum has, but she will be back Saturday." Basically, Tia could stay there. I read the message to Tia. She jumped off the kitchen side. She ran – "yes, yes, yes, yes, yes" – and, all of a sudden, she came behind me, put her arms around me. I leaned over, gave her a kiss on the head and off she went.'

Natalie Sharp had not seen or heard from her daughter since then. Between sobs she added, 'This is hell – I'm beginning to fear the worst. It's a nightmare. Tia's just a normal girl, not a runaway. She's loved, missed and wanted by everybody. I just want my little girl back.'

Detective Chief Inspector Robin Bhairam from Croydon Police, who was leading the investigation at the time, told the press, 'We still we have no news on her whereabouts. I reiterate our appeals for anyone who may have seen Tia, or has information about her, to come forward. Of course, if Tia herself can contact her family or the police, we urge her to do so. Her family are very concerned as this is wholly out of character.'

Detective Chief Inspector Nick Scola, of Scotland Yard,

added that they had 'received a number of purported sightings but none has been confirmed'. By that time there had been 55. The last person known to have seen her was her grandmother's partner, he said. Meanwhile, police continued their house-to-house inquiries and residents handed out flyers.

On Sunday night, 5 August, Tia's 28-year-old uncle David Sharp made an emotional appeal. 'At this stage, it's a relatively simple timeline as we know,' he said. 'She was at her grandmother's address, she slept late and then she left to get the bus. We've had one neighbour who's reported possibly seeing her walking to the bus stop but as yet that is uncorroborated. Tia's a 12-year-old normal girl. She has never run away, she's got no reason to run away. She's a playful child, she's not an adult… but she's very clued-up in travelling and local areas and people she knows.'

Speaking at a press conference at Scotland Yard, he said, 'I just want to say to Tia, "I want you to come home. You are not in any trouble."'

Already the family and friends were organising a publicity campaign. Mr Sharp and the two friends accompanying him were wearing T-shirts with Tia's picture on it under the word 'MISSING'. The shirts also carried an appeal:

12 YEAR OLD TIA SHARP
LAST SEEN AROUND 1 PM ON FRIDAY 3RD AUGUST
IN NEW ADDINGTON/CROYDON
WEARING YELLOW TOP, GREY TROUSERS
AND BLACK AND PINK TRAINERS.
IF ANYONE HAS ANY INFORMATION PLEASE RING

It then gave the phone number for a local search centre and 999 for the police. While leaflets were being distributed carrying the same message, the campaign was also being waged through social-networking websites. By then more than 7,000 people had visited a Facebook site set up to help search for her. Her pictures showed her wearing her spectacles and looking younger than her 12 years, or trying to appear older without them. In one, she was cheekily sticking out her tongue, which was painted blue. Another showed her looking serious, dressed in her school uniform.

CHAPTER TWO

VIGIL

That Sunday night a candlelit vigil was held in New Addington by the army of local residents who had posted thousands of leaflets through letterboxes to help publicise the search. As darkness fell on The Lindens, a group of about 20 relatives and friends carried candles from Tia grandmother's terraced house in New Addington and placed them at intervals along the street where she would have walked towards the main road, 'to light her way home'. And at the bus stop nearby, well-wishers left dozens of other candles and tea lights with hand-written signs asking for Tia to be brought home.

Tia's uncle David Sharp told the crowd, 'I want to say thank you to the police for doing everything that they can, and the public for their support and being out there day and night. I urge you not to stop. I want Tia found, so please do what you're doing.'

While detectives continued to sift through hours of CCTV footage, the best they could come up with was a grainy image from the Co-op store in Featherbed Lane, New Addington at 4.15pm on Thursday, 2 August, the day before she went missing. It showed her wearing a yellow vest with the picture of an animal on the front and leggings – an outfit similar to the one she was wearing when she went missing. However, the footage showed her wearing Ugg boots, which she was thought to have swapped for black Nike trainers with a pink swoosh when she disappeared.

The store had up to 16 cameras and she was seen walking and playing in the aisles on Thursday afternoon. She was seen with a 'family member' and they spent £40 on groceries before leaving. Tia was said to have been happy, smiling and giggling while in the shop.

It was then announced that the last person to see her was her grandmother's boyfriend, 37-year-old window cleaner Stuart Hazell, who Tia called Granddad. He told the police that Tia had got up late and left the couple's home in New Addington at midday on Friday to travel by bus to The Whitgift Centre in Croydon. However, there were conflicting reports about Hazell's story and whether he last saw her at the house or not. It turned out he had told his dad Keith that he took Tia down to the local tram station after lending her £11 to buy flip-flops.

Keith Hazell told the *Daily Mirror*, 'I spoke to him on the phone and he told me he walked her down to Addington tram station to get the tram to Croydon. He didn't see her get on but he took her down there to the station.'

Then, according to Hazell senior, his son said she set off

alone for The Whitgift Centre three miles away without her phone, travel card or coat, and with just the £11 he had lent her.

The police were convinced that she had gone no further than Croydon and, as specialist search teams continued to comb the area, Tia's grandmother, 47-year-old Christine Bicknell, a care support worker, also talked to the press. She said she was at work that day.

'Tia promised that she would be home by six,' Christine told the *Mirror*. 'I've still got her dinner in the oven. It's pizza and chips and I can't bear to take it out.'

She said she could not understand why her grand-daughter had not been seen after she left her council house. 'There were workmen here on the estate, yet nobody saw her leave,' she said.

However, the situation was a little more complicated than she had made out. In an interview with *Sky News*, she said, 'I was at work but Tia was in the house with her granddad. He said she was going to catch the bus to go shopping in Croydon. It's a journey she's done before but not on her own.'

Other puzzling aspects of the case showed themselves when another version of Hazell's story emerged in the press.

Step-father David Niles's mother, 69-year-old Angie Niles, told the *Mirror*, 'Apparently, Stuart was doing the housework work and hoovering or something when Tia shouted, "I'm going out, I'm going to meet so-and-so." But he didn't catch who she said she was going to meet. By the time he thought about it, she'd left the house. That was the last anyone saw of her.'

A retired mum of four, Angie Niles also lived in Mitcham, not far from her son, Natalie, Tia and the two boys. She also said she was baffled as to why Tia had not taken her phone with her when she left her grandmother's house.

'I can't understand why she wouldn't have her phone with her because, when she used to come around here, she'd sit there with the phone glued to her ear,' she said. 'She was always messaging her friends. I've heard that it was on charge but that's so strange to me because, when she stayed at mine, she would charge it at night.'

Angie Niles then said she has had a gut feeling that something bad had happened to her beloved step-granddaughter. Weeping, she said, 'I've had a terrible feeling right from Friday night that she's not going to turn up. She's gone; I know she is. She's either been abducted or... I don't know, I just don't know.'

At that point she broke down. Other people had had similar feelings. Few now, after so much time had passed, expected Tia to return unscathed.

'My gut feeling is that she never left New Addington,' said Angie, composing herself. 'If they're going to find her, it will be there. If she got on that tram to Croydon there would be CCTV of it.'

According to Mrs Niles, Tia saw her step-father David as her dad after he moved in with her mum eight years before. Her biological father, 30-year-old sign fitter Steven Carter, left Tia's mother Natalie soon after Tia was born and had moved to Northampton 10 years before. Nevertheless, Carter, who has Tia's name tattooed on his right forearm, travelled to New Addington that weekend to join the search for his missing daughter. 'We're all working together to try to find her,' he said.

Mrs Niles added that Tia regularly stayed with her grandmother and her boyfriend but had stopped doing so as much in recent months. Later she would explain why.

Updating the press, Detective Chief Inspector Nick Scola said, 'At this stage, it's a relatively simple timeline as we know. She was at her grandmother's address, she slept late and then she left to get the bus. We have had one neighbour who's reported possibly seeing her walking to the bus stop but as yet that is uncorroborated. I am appealing for any bus or tram drivers in the Croydon area who recognise Tia's description to contact us. Of course, if Tia herself is able to contact her family or the police, we urge her to do so.'

DCI Scola said that Tia was not known to have a boyfriend and that there were no indications that she was having any trouble at her secondary school. She had never gone missing before. Officers were seen searching garages close to her grandmother's house and, he said, they had plenty of leads to follow up.

'We have had 55 sightings of Tia,' said Scola. 'They are being investigated but as yet we can't substantiate any of them.'

The police were also still looking for a man in a white van or Vauxhall Corsa who had been hassling children in the area at the time Tia vanished. They could not 'substantiate' this claim but did not rule out the line of inquiry. By then the investigation had been handed over to Scotland Yard's homicide and serious-crime command. They had sent specialist police teams to search gardens and school grounds close to Tia's grandmother's home. A team of nine officers dressed in blue police baseball hats and black coats used long sticks to scour the undergrowth.

That Tuesday, 7 August, the *Sun* was offering £25,000 for information that might lead the police to the missing girl. A local shopkeeper offered another £500.

When told of the *Sun*'s appeal, Tia's step-father David Niles said, 'If you want to do that, it's very much appreciated. I'd love you to do that.'

Angie Niles said, 'I hope your offer of a reward will work. If anybody can tell me any information, I'll be so grateful. I can't believe this is happening.'

On behalf of the police, DCI Nick Scola said of the reward, 'We are very grateful for any support. Our focus is on finding Tia. We support the appeal and urge anyone with information to come forward to police.'

Local volunteers moved the centre of their operations to Croydon Rugby Club where they gathered before setting out on the search. Club secretary Sue Randall told the press, 'We were here last night with the police and they told us all to come back today. At the moment there are about a hundred people but more came and went off to start the search.'

David Niles, wearing a Find Tia campaign T-shirt, said, 'I just want to find my little girl. How would you feel if it was your daughter? We're in bits. The whole country has helped us and is supporting us. I haven't slept in four days. Natalie is in bits. The police have done everything. I know I am not her real dad but I have been there since day dot.' Niles continued, 'I have fed her and bathed her. I just want her home. When she left the house, she shouted, "Bye!" and, "See you by six.'"

Christine Bicknell was back in the press, saying she hoped the image of her granddaughter taken outside the nearby Co-op on Thursday and released by the police that Monday would jog people's memories and bring forward new information. She also thanked the community for supporting the family and helping in the search. By then a solitary candle was being left in the street, burning in a glass holder with a plastic bottle covering it.

Also on Tuesday, Tia's mother Natalie finally faced the press: 'My baby girl walked out and she vanished,' she told the *Croydon Advertiser*. 'We all feel terrible. We think she's been taken but we just don't know. There is no CCTV. We know absolutely nothing. I wish to God I could tell you something.'

She said a woman had seen her leave Tia's grandmother's house alone: 'I have an independent witness [said] that she left on her own walking down the road.'

Natalie went on to pose for a poster as part of the *Sun*'s £25,000 appeal, saying, 'Please help us find her.'

She and her boyfriend David Niles said they had not given up hope. Meanwhile, it was reported that footballer Wayne Rooney had joined the search, retweeting an appeal poster.

By then the family were showing signs of strain. The police had been taking an interest in Christine Bicknell's boyfriend, Stuart Hazell, who was still the last person to have had a confirmed sighting of Tia. Hazell was well known to the police. He had spent three years in jail for supplying crack cocaine in 2003 and then met Christine after being released from prison in 2010 following a second conviction for the possession of a machete. After his release, Hazell had dated Natalie before starting a relationship with her mother Christine, police said.

Stuart's father Keith said, 'Stuart is very close to Tia. She used to call him Granddad. He was like a dad and a granddad to her. He'd have done anything for her.'

According to Keith Hazell, his son was greatly distressed by Tia's disappearance. 'He is absolutely heartbroken,' said Keith. 'Where has she gone?'

Fearing the worst, the police continued combing a wood less than a mile from where she was last seen.

Tia's disappearance remained a mystery. Nevertheless, the family made every effort to keep the fate of the missing schoolgirl in the public eye in the face of the massive coverage being given to the Olympic Games. Flanked by Christine Bicknell, David Niles faced the cameras once again to say, 'There is nothing to go on, she just came out of here, went that way and disappeared. The police are doing the best they can. I am more interested in my little girl. It is a hard time for me and my family; we haven't heard from the police today.

'We are hoping, we just want her to come back. Imagine if it was your little girl missing. We've done everything possible. We are just going to keep looking for her, just keep appealing and get out there. I haven't slept for four days and nor has her mum Natalie. I am just praying. The police asked us to keep chatting to people, keep thinking what she could have done.' He added that Tia 'was good as gold' when he'd last seen her, when he left for work on the previous Thursday.

Niles also made an appeal on Facebook, saying, 'Its daddy. Plz cum home I love u and miss u xxxxxxxxxxx.'

While hopes faded, Tia's biological father Steven Carter said he believed she was still alive, insisting that he would know if something had happened to her. But he had not attended the candlelit vigil. 'At the candle lighting for Tia, David Niles lit the candle for me,' he said. 'We're good friends and he was the one who told me this was happening.'

However, he found the idea of a vigil disturbing. 'Candles for me mean death,' he said. 'So I blew mine out. When she is home and safe I'll relight mine.'

Despite the rumours that were now circulating, he did not want to point any finger of blame, adding, 'It's all Chinese whispers. What matters is she comes home safe.'

On the other hand, Christine Bicknell's partner Stuart Hazell was said to be inconsolable. His sister Sarah Parratt told friends, 'My brother keeps breaking down. He's struggling to cope.'

However, Hazell had been seen being led on Wednesday, 8 August from Christine's house by two men in plain clothes. He was put in a car and driven away. The police said that he was being interviewed as a witness and had not been arrested. A police dog was also seen being taken into the premises.

CHAPTER THREE

THE SEARCH

The search for Tia was stepped up when, as this was fast becoming a very serious investigation with a major media following, Metropolitan Police Commissioner Bernard Hogan-Howe visited the incident room in south London and spoke to officers viewing hundreds of hours of CCTV footage in an attempt to trace her last steps.

A police spokesman later said, 'We have collected more than 800 hours so far of CCTV footage from buses, trams, and we have viewed more than 120 hours of that,' adding that it was a 24/7 process and that police would continue to collect more CCTV footage. 'It is incredibly time-consuming but it is a vital line of inquiry.'

Another 80 officers were redirected from Olympics duties to join the hunt – 40 detectives and 40 specialist search officers. Searches covered a 500-metre radius around Tia's grandmother's house, including woodland, garages, lock-ups, a local school and bins on the estate, using sticks to scour through the rubbish. However, the police stressed that the investigation remained a missing-person inquiry, not a murder case.

Metropolitan Police area chief for south-east London, Borough Commander Neil Basu, found it easy to empathise. His eldest son had gone missing at a similar age. However, the child was only gone for two hours. 'It was, still is, the worst two hours of my life,' said Basu to the press. 'I can't imagine how it must feel for this family after five days. The family want Tia home. They miss her dreadfully.'

He said that Scotland Yard had received more than 300 calls and that there had been some 60 reported sightings of Tia, including one person who came forward to say they'd seen Tia leaving her grandmother's house alone at about noon on the day she disappeared. A female neighbour also gave a signed statement saying that she had seen Tia leaving on her own. However, Besu added that they could not be 'absolutely sure' who the last person to see Tia on the estate was. Again he stressed that the investigation remained a missing-persons inquiry. There were, as yet, no suspects. 'I am looking to find Tia safe and well,' he said.

However, he did not feel the schoolgirl would have left the area and the search was, at that time, focused only on the neighbourhood and Croydon, where Tia had been thought to be heading. Commander Basu said that the Alsatian that people had seen being taken into Tia's grandmother's house was one of the 'specialist resources' being used to help find the youngster.

He went on to thank the people from the Croydon and

Mitcham areas, and praised those involved in the search for Tia for their 'generosity, their energy and their commitment'. The volunteers had donned 'Find Tia' T-shirts and handed out thousands of leaflets to passing drivers. Hundreds had also searched nearby fields, under police supervision.

The local pub, the Randall Tavern, had a leaflet appealing for help pinned to the bar. 'Whatever people say about New Addington, it's a nice area,' said landlord Peter Wilson. 'I've run pubs on this estate for 16 years. It's a close-knit place and people have really come together.'

The area had experienced other problems over the past year and a Co-op store about a mile from where Tia went missing was attacked during the riots in 2011. However, the Randall Tavern had remained open during the disturbances and a hundred people came in to defend the local shops from damage. 'They were saying, "They are not going to mess with our pub." It's all down to community spirit,' he said. 'We've just now all got to hope that the young girl is alive.'

Other areas were taped off while police dogs and their handlers went about their business and a helicopter flew above. The candlelit vigil continued. That evening, the evening of the Wednesday, three young girls were seen lighting candles at the bus stop where Tia was supposed to have taken the bus to Croydon. Nearby there was an appeal for Tia to come home chalked on the pavement.

Meanwhile, officers with a sniffer dog spent 20 minutes searching Tia's grandmother's council house. At the time, her boyfriend Stuart Hazell had been taken away by two detectives and was adding to his witness statement at the local police station. A Scotland Yard spokesman said he had not been arrested and he was later released.

The following day came more disturbing news. The *Daily Mirror* revealed that Christine Bicknell had told detectives that she had not seen the schoolgirl in the 24 hours before her disappearance. Previously it had been thought that Bicknell had spent the evening with Tia and Hazell at her home. However, she now said that she had been out overnight on Thursday, working as a carer, and that she did not return home until late the following afternoon, after Tia had vanished. And the family member seen with Tia in the Co-op in New Addington was said to be Hazell. She then returned with him by bus to her grandmother's home, it was said.

Although Hazell had been taken to the police station twice by this stage, Tia's uncle David Sharp said that the family was sure he had nothing to do with Tia's disappearance. Minutes after Hazell had been led away by officers for the third time, David Sharp wrote on the Help Find Tia page on Facebook, 'Stuart has done nothing wrong. The police are doing their job. He just has to make a formal statement, that's all. So stop pointing your finger, we're not the sick family you're trying to make out. If you're not willing to help find Tia leave this site.'

He also attacked the 'sick trolls' that were targeting the website. But the rumours persisted.

However, the police insisted that Hazell had attended the police station voluntarily as a witness. He left the house on 8 August under the full glare of press and television cameras but would not answer reporters' questions. He was then seen being driven away in a black Vauxhall Astra.

Hazell was interviewed for two and a half hours before being returned home at 8pm that night. Nevertheless, the police insisted that he was not a suspect. But Angie Niles was still concerned about the discrepancies between Hazell's story and the tale he had told his father Keith about walking her down to the tram station to get the tram to Croydon, believing that these might have hampered the chances of finding her. It seems that these were aspects that detectives also wanted to clarify.

Meanwhile, sniffer dogs returned to the woods – and to the house where Hazell lived with Tia's grandmother. The search units were concentrating on a 500-metre zone around Ms Sharp's house. They were searching garages, gardens, school grounds, skips and parks. Police from the West Yorkshire team who had investigated the disappearance of Shannon Matthews – the Dewsbury schoolgirl kidnapped by her own mother and her former boyfriend's uncle – were called in to aid the inquiry. Scotland Yard said they had been drafted in for their expertise in kidnap cases, in particular the disappearance of nine-year-old Shannon. Karen Matthews and her accomplice Michael Donovan were convicted in December 2008 of her kidnap, which they had committed to claim a £50,000 in reward. The girl had been drugged and imprisoned for 24 days.

'As is routine, we liaise with all forces that have dealt with similar cases,' said a spokesman for the Metropolitan Police. 'This case is like the Shannon Matthews case. This is a missing-persons case and we are putting all our resources into finding her.'

However, detectives made it clear that there was no

evidence that Tia's abduction had been faked by the family, as had been in the Shannon Matthews' case. Senior officers were said to be angry at the inference, saying that it could hamper the investigation into Tia's disappearance.

The conjecture was shrugged off by the family. David Sharp still managed to keep a brave face: 'Everyone is trying to do their best by sticking together and keeping everything tight and supporting each other,' he told the press. 'I don't know what has happened to Tia. I don't want anyone to think the worst has happened to Tia.'

He said he hoped she was 'somewhere safe' and begged her, 'Come home. There is no trouble. Walk through that door.' He also said that he was amazed by the support being given by members of the public who were helping in the search.

Former detective and child-protection expert Mark Williams-Thomas was called in to support the family. After suspicion fell on him, Hazell asked if he could make an appeal for the safe return of Tia. As a result, Williams-Thomas conducted an interview for ITV News in the house in New Addington where Tia had disappeared. It was broadcast on Thursday, 9 August.

Sitting on the sofa at his home in New Addington, Hazell became quite emotional during questioning. He was accompanied by David Sharp. Both wore white 'Find Tia' T-shirts and a large picture of her hung on the wall behind them.

Williams-Thomas asked Hazell if Tia had had any problems at home.

'She's got no problems at all,' said Hazell. 'She's a happy-go-lucky golden angel. You know what I mean? She's perfect. There's no arguments, no nothing. Nothing we could think of, absolutely nothing.'

Hazell then seized the opportunity to make a direct appeal to Tia.

'Just come home, babe, come and eat your dinner,' he said. 'I want my £10 back for the garden. I want things back to normal. I want to find her in McDonald's, sitting there spending my tenner.'

Williams-Thomas knew that the police would be looking at Hazell because he was the last person to see Tia. He wanted to hear Hazell's account of what had happened first-hand, and asked Hazell to talk him through the last time he had seen Tia.

Hazell said that Tia had come downstairs at about 10.30 or 11am and was playing with her Nintendo DS while he tidied up. 'She'd been going on about going to Croydon and getting up early,' he said. 'She came downstairs, sat down, watched telly, played the DS.'

Hazell said he asked her if she wanted any breakfast and made some toast. 'She had toast, then wanted a sausage roll – she was always eating sausage rolls,' he said. 'Then she didn't take her washing-up out, so I took her washing-up out. I started doing a bit of washing-up and she was telling me what she was doing but I wasn't really logging it. It didn't – you know what I mean – kids, they talk to you, it goes in one ear, stays there for a second, and it goes out, you know what I mean?'

He said he'd been vacuuming when she went out. 'She walked passed me from the front room to go out,' she said. 'And she walked out the front door. That is all I know. And she left her [bleep] phone on charge.'

He went on to explain that he had told her to leave her phone on charge but that he had not meant her to leave it behind: 'What Tia is doing, she plays on the BB [BBM, BlackBerry Messenger] thing but she uses it as it is charging, so there is no charge going through to it. So when I said to her, "Leave your phone on charge," it means leave your phone on charge, let it charge up a bit then you can actually take with you or do whatever.'

Although she had only just turned 12, Tia had been to Croydon on her own before, he said. She was responsible enough to go on trains and buses and trams on her own.

Williams-Thomas asked if she had said anything as she left.

Hazell replied, 'She said, "Goodbye," and I said, "Make sure you are back at six." She went, "Yeah, yeah, yeah." And that was it. The door closed and she walked out. I don't take precise times and things like that. But when she walked out of that door, I know damn well that was ten past twelve, according to my clock. Because I was hoovering up the dog's mess by the kitchen. And I look up and there is a great big clock in front of me on the cooker which says twelve-ten.'

Hazell had essentially been under house arrest for seven days, Williams-Thomas said.

'It's been horrible, horrible, you know what I mean?' Hazell responded. 'The family's stuck inside here. I mean we've got all those papers outside all putting accusations down. And they ask me stupid questions. Yesterday, like, "Did you do anything?" Well, no, I bloody didn't. Excuse my language. But I didn't. I would never think of that. I loved her to bits. She was like my own daughter. For God's sake. We had that sort of relationship. We were that sort of thing. It was just – you know – she wanted it, she got it. She's got a loving home. She has never gone without anything. So I can't work it out. What the hell's going on? They're all out there. They want to report the truth.'

Did Hazell feel under pressure? Did he feel that people were looking at him with suspicion?

'Well, if they believe what they read in the papers, they can do whatever they like,' he said. 'I know deep down in my heart that Tia walked out of my house. She walked out of there. I know damn well because she was seen walking down the pathway. I know she made that track down that way. What happened after that I don't know.'

Then he made a fresh appeal. 'Tia come home, babes – come back.'

David Sharp lent his support to Hazell on camera.

'We just need the people out there to stop pointing their fingers because he is feeling it hard as it is, as you know,' he said. 'It's hard enough on him as it is. We don't need no more added stress. We need Tia found. If they want to help us in any kind of way, don't point the finger. Find her. Then point the finger. When we've found her, point the finger saying, "There she is." That is all we want.'

Hazell then put his arm around David.

Williams-Thomas was not convinced by what he saw. He knew that Hazell was telling friends that he believed Tia had been snatched by a paedophile so, after the interview, in the kitchen, Williams-Thomas asked Hazell what he thought had happened to Tia. He replied, 'I think a nonce has got her.'

His partner Christine Bicknell admitted on several occasions that Hazell had a 'shady past'. He had more than

30 convictions for crimes including theft, burglary, handling stolen goods, dealing crack cocaine and a machete attack. But she insisted that he would do nothing to harm the girl who she said he 'loves to bits'.

Questioned about his criminal record during the interview, Hazell said people should not judge him on his record. 'My previous has got nothing to do with it,' he said. 'Everyone's got a shady past. Did I do anything to Tia? No, I bloody didn't. I'd never think of that.'

The night before she vanished they were alone together in the house, he said, eating pizza and chips and playing computer games. However, according to grandmother Christine, the pizza and chips were still in the oven and she could not bear to throw food way.

The interview with Hazell received wide currency in the press. He'd explained that Christine had been out that night, working as a carer. She had not seen Tia on the Thursday or Friday when she vanished.

He'd insisted that it was exactly 12.10pm when she got up to go. And that she had told him previously she wanted to go to Croydon to buy some new shoes with the £10 he had given her for tidying up the garden and doing a few chores around the house.

Questions were being asked – why did she not take her mobile phone with her? It was left on charge, something she usually did overnight. Even though she intended to take public transport, she did not take her travel card with her. Nor did the young lady carry a handbag. She did not even have a set of keys with her but Hazell had said he planned to be in when she returned.

Hazell claimed he was busy and distracted at the time

she left, and that now he kicked himself for not paying more attention. He had told police that, as she was leaving, Tia had mentioned the name of a friend that she was meeting but he did not hear it.

Even before the interview, the finger of suspicion was being turned upon him and he blamed certain sections of the media. 'They just twist your words,' he said. 'If they laid off us a bit, I could actually be out there looking, I want to be out there looking myself but I'm stuck in here like a prisoner. I feel helpless.'

He said he was confident a neighbour who told police he saw Tia leave the house was genuine. She was a family friend who knew Tia well and had even been able to describe 'the pattern on her top'. He said he knew what Tia was wearing when she left the house that morning.

'She was wearing exactly what she had when she came up here because I washed her clothes that night,' said Hazell. 'It was a yellow, one of them tight tube things, grey – like jeans but they weren't jeans – leggings?'

The witness said she had spotted Tia near her grandmother's house. It was 12.10pm and she was walking on her own towards a bus stop. A second witness was also said to have seen her. Hazell said that she was on her way to catch the 231 bus into Croydon, a journey that she had made many times before. The witness said that she was certain it had been Tia she'd seen that Friday. The police were treating the witness as a credible source and were following up the sighting. However, after combing through hours of CCTV footage, the police had begun to suspect that she never got on the bus, casting doubt on Hazell's story that she had gone to Croydon.

Again Hazell struck back at what he perceived to be a media campaign against him and the people who thought he had something to do with Tia's disappearance. He was being blamed wrongly, he said, during the same interview. 'I do feel that people are pointing the finger at me 'cause till the other day it was known that I was the last person to see her but I wasn't. It's not about me, it's about Tia and we've got to get her home, man.'

However, the interview with ITV News didn't seem to help him in the way he'd hoped. In it, he looked nervous and shifty. And it was not the press that was against him – it was the general public.

'I think after the interview it was quite clear that people began to wonder whether what we had been told was the truth,' Hannah Wilson of the *Croydon Guardian* said. 'On the social networking sites, people began to draw their own conclusions and were saying quite freely that they thought he was lying, that they didn't believe his version of events, that his eyes, his facial expression, certain things about that interview gave away to them that he wasn't quite being truthful.'

Hazell was plainly fighting a losing battle. Tia's family were still backing him but his father – his own flesh and blood – certainly hadn't helped the situation.

He dismissed claims that his father Keith had contradicted his version of events by saying that his son had walked her to the tram stop. 'My dad likes a drink,' Hazell said. 'He's got good intentions but he said everything back to front. If I'd have walked her to the tram stop, I would have come with her to Croydon, then none of this would have happened.'

They had travelled by tram the previous day. Hazell said he'd met Tia at East Croydon at 4pm. Together they had taken the tram back to New Addington where they spent the evening on the PlayStation. This was 'nothing unusual', he said, "cause she's cheating all the time.'

The police were taking renewed interest in Hazell. DCI Nick Scola, now leading the investigation, visited Tia's grandmother's home in New Addington on the night of the interview, spending 40 minutes there.

'We're here to speak to Tia's family and offer our support at this very difficult time,' he said when he emerged. 'We are updating them on the investigation and want to reassure them that we are desperate to find Tia and are supporting them in their efforts.'

However, other officers removed possessions from the house in evidence bags. One was tagged 'duvet'. Police still confined their search to within 500 metres, emptying bins and checking lock-up garages. But they had also cordoned off a landfill site where the rubbish collected from the 2,000 houses on the estate was dumped.

The following day, Christine Bicknell was also taken in for questioning. A Smart car drove her to the police station, where she was interviewed for two hours. It was said that she was questioned as a witness and that there was no suggestion she had had anything to do with Tia's disappearance. When she returned around 2.30pm carrying a box of washing powder and two packets of cigarettes, she made no comment to waiting reporters.

When Christine made it through the press pack, she was distraught and sobbing. Hazell played the role of a concerned partner, breaking off an interview to comfort her. 'The press are bombarding her down there on her own,' he complained. 'They won't let her park the car… It's hitting her hard. She come up on her own.'

Forensic psychologist Kerry Daynes later explained the crucial role that Christine Bicknell played: 'Christine is the matriarch of the family and she feels that she's got to put a brave face on it for everybody else. You really see that when she leaves the safety of the home and she goes into the press pack. And so, of course, we've seen photos of her looking, frankly, quite fierce and hostile. But, underneath that, there's a very vulnerable side to Christine, which, of course, the press haven't got to see. And a very frightened side as well.'

By then over a week had passed since Tia's disappearance, and Metropolitan Police Commander Neil Basu was still saying that he couldn't be 'absolutely sure' who had been the last person to see Tia on the estate. This seemed to cast doubt on the witnesses who'd said that they'd seen Tia after she left her grandmother's house on her way to the bus stop. However, the investigation remained a missing-persons case, not a murder inquiry. As a consequence, at this point, there were no suspects.

Later, Natalie Sharp described how she'd felt as the search continued.

'As the days passed, the range of emotions we went through was like nothing I can describe,' she told the *Daily Mail*. 'I've tried to tell people, to put my finger on it, but I can't. You feel empty, like you're being twisted from the inside. All the way from your stomach to your throat.'

The worry began to have a physical effect on her.

'You can't eat, you can't sleep,' she said. 'It's horrible, I wouldn't wish it on my worst enemy… All we could do was wait, and waiting is the hardest part, because what else can you do? But the more you wait, the more you know in your heart of hearts that it's not going to happen. It's the last thing you think about when you go to bed at night and the first thing you think about when you wake up. It's still that way now. I remember, every day she was missing, I'd wake up and open my eyes and things felt normal for a second or maybe two. But then there was this kick in your stomach when you realised where you were and what was happening.'

CHAPTER FOUR

MANHUNT

Then on the evening of Friday, 10 August, news came that Tia's body had been found in her grandmother's house – the very house from which Stuart Hazell had made his emotional appeal for her return on television the night before. It then emerged that the police had searched the house several times before the body was discovered. What's more, Stuart Hazell had gone missing.

Commander Neil Basu admitted that four searches had been made of the property but defended the police actions. 'When the police investigate cases as difficult and challenging as this,' he said, 'it is important that we do not just focus on one line of inquiry. For example, we had over 60 reported sightings of Tia, 800 hours of CCTV footage to examine and 300 plus calls in the incident room. All of these lines of inquiry were in the process of being followed up.'

Then he gave details of what had happened at the house in New Addington.

'A number of searches took place at the address. When Tia was first reported missing, officers searched her bedroom, as is normal practice in a missing-persons inquiry. A further search of the house took place in the early hours of Sunday morning by a specialist team. This was then followed by another search of the house by specialist dogs on Wednesday lunchtime. What we now need to establish is how long the body had been in the place where it was found. This will be [the] subject of the ongoing investigation and it would be wrong to jump to any conclusions until all the facts have been established.'

Throughout the inquiry, Commander Basu and his officers had worked closely with Tia's family. 'We have kept them updated and have provided support at all times,' he said. 'The pre-planned search was undertaken with their full cooperation. Our priority now is to establish the facts of the case and, to assist us with this, we are keen to speak to all those people who last saw Tia.'

Police would not reveal where the body was discovered but officers had been seen taking a ladder into the property that afternoon, sparking rumours that it was in the loft. Later, a dark holdall was seen being removed from the house.

Shortly before the fateful search began, Christine Bicknell had left the house wearing a T-shirt appealing for the return of her granddaughter and broken down as she spoke about Tia's disappearance. 'My only message to Tia is that I love her,' said Bicknell. 'She is my life. I don't know where she has gone. I don't know how she's gone but she's not staying away by choice, I know this. I will help the police and everybody else every way I can, so will every one of my family. I just want my baby back.'

She told reporters that Hazell was helping with the search. 'We've all done our own little separate bit and Stuart's out doing that now,' she said. Asked what he was doing, she said, 'I don't know, I don't know where he is. He is out doing his own thing.'

She asked for understanding: 'Whatever way he is, he has had it hard. He knows the finger has been pointed at him. He knows this and it's been really hard for him.'

She then invited the press to return when Tia was found safe and well. 'I hope you are all here to see me strangle her,' she joked. 'When she gets home, I want to kill her.'

Earlier that morning, two women detectives had arrived at Mrs Bicknell's house. Thirty minutes later, they left with brown evidence bags. Plainly something had been found. Sniffer dogs were brought in and Mrs Bicknell left the house with an officer at noon. An hour later, the police sealed off the area for a 'pre-arranged search'. Later, the police said they had found the body at 4.45pm, and the grim announcement that a body had been found at 20 The Lindens, New Addington followed soon after. Then it was announced that a murder inquiry was underway.

Local people congregated near the scene. They expressed shock when they heard the news that a body had been found and tempers flared. A neighbour, 40-year-old Eileen Minogue, said that residents on the close-knit estate felt 'betrayed'. 'We've been searching woodland,' she said. 'We've spent two nights in the rain searching woodland, delivering leaflets. I feel disgusted. It is heartbreaking.'

Nevertheless, she felt compassion for Tia's relatives: 'I feel for the genuine family – Tia's mum Natalie, the cousins and aunts – who have been in that house having sleepless nights. I have just seen one of her cousins collapsing. I can't imagine how they feel.'

Another neighbour, 32-year-old Alston Millington, said she had still been hoping for the best. 'Personally, I was hoping she had a bit of trouble at home and had run off, rebelling against the family maybe,' she said. 'I was hoping she would be found somewhere with somebody.'

However, she had known that it was a futile hope.

'It is very hard to get out of Addington without being seen in either a car, tram or bus,' she said. 'It is such sad news. I live just around the corner and can't believe it. I think it's disgusting. Everybody around here knew she wasn't far from the house. It makes me sick.'

Christine Bicknell and other relatives gathered in a park near Addington police station after the discovery of Tia. Her real grandfather and Christine's ex (the couple had divorced 14 years previously after having 2 children, David and Tia's mother Natalie), Paul Sharp, said, 'A piece of my heart has been torn out'

A manhunt was launched for Stuart Hazell and people were warned not to approach him: 'Following a search of the property this afternoon, we are seeking to find Stuart Hazell to be interviewed in connection with this case,' said a spokesman for the Met. 'He should not be approached and, if seen, people should call 999 immediately. There have been no arrests in connection with this investigation at this time. The family of Tia Sharp has been informed of the discovery.'

Neighbour Emma McKay said, 'To be honest, I am relieved that it does not seem to be a stranger who has snatched a kid off the streets. I am sure someone will find Stuart Hazell.'

Just an hour after the body was found, Hazell was spotted buying booze in nearby Morden, south London. The off-licence's CCTV shows him in a shop wearing a dark baseball cap, blue polo shirt and a grey hoodie. According to the shopkeeper, 49-year old Prasanna Jayakumar, Hazell said, 'Help me find Tia, I can't sleep without her.'

It was just after 5pm.

Jayakumar said, 'He came in and was very drunk, swaying all over the place and saying, "I'm Tia's granddad and I need to find her." He was crying and hitting his head with his fists. I didn't realise who he was and felt quite sorry for him. He pointed to a poster we have of Tia and said, "I'm looking for her."'

According to Jayakumar, he came in twice and bought a half-bottle of Glen's vodka and a lighter on both occasions. The two visits were about six minutes apart.

She recognised Hazell, whose mother lives nearby, but did not connect him to the murder hunt. 'It was the little girl Chloe who was buying sweets in the shop who said he was wanted for Tia's murder,' said Jayakumar.

11-year-old schoolgirl Chloe Bird was terrified when she came face-to-face with Hazell. She said told the press that she was in the Cannon Hill Lane mini-market buying sweets when a drunken Hazell burst in. 'He walked in and he was buying some alcohol and a lighter,' she said, 'and he was telling the lady behind the counter that he wanted to find Tia and that he wanted her back. Then he turned around to me and said, if I find Tia, can I tell her to come back, please.'

Chloe recognised him from the TV and knew he was on the run.

'I knew it was Tia's granddad and he scared me,' she said. 'He was crying and saying how much he missed Tia. He looked drunk.'

She told the BBC, 'He was in the shop buying some alcohol and a lighter and he was crying to the lady behind the counter, and he was saying, "I want Tia back, I miss her so much", and then he turned around to me and said, "Do you know Tia?" and I said, "Tia Sharp?" and he said, "Yes, do you know where she is?" and I said, "No, sorry."'

Suspicious, Jayakumar looked in a newspaper to check that it was really Hazell but he had already left the shop. 'He went out and started talking to people and they called the police,' Jayakumar said.

Passer-by Chris Watkins, a 52-year-old heating engineer, also spotted the fugitive. 'I saw him outside the shops walking away from me just after 5pm,' he said, and managed to engage him in conversation. 'He said he was going over to Joseph Wood to look for Tia,' Mr Watkins said. 'The next thing, the police were here but he wasn't. For about two hours there were police cars up and down our streets looking for him. They had a trail bike and a patrol car driving over the common but he had disappeared.'

After their brief conversation, Chloe Bird had run across the road to get away. Once home, she confirmed his identity by watching the TV news before telling her step-father, 41-year-old Nicholas Keeley, that she had spotted Hazell. 'I was crying and shaking,' she said. 'I rang my nan and told her and she said, "Call the police." My step-dad thought he was already with the police so it could not be him. But I told them I was sure and he rang 999.'

Keeley was quickly on his mobile. The call was logged at 5.39pm.

'The police were here within five minutes,' he said. 'I hadn't even finished telling them where he was and they were here. There were like five cars within five minutes and then the whole area was swarmed with police.'

They interviewed Chloe, who was still shaking.

'I was quite scared. I am still a bit scared,' she said. 'The police wanted to know what was he wearing and, how did he seem? Was he drunk? I told them he was crying and what he had said to me. He came up and asked me if I knew Tia. I said, "Tia Sharp?" and he said, "Yes, I'm her granddad, I'm looking for her. Do you know her?" I said, "Yes," meaning that I knew her but he thought I was saying I knew where she was.'

Carrying his drink, Hazell had stumbled into the Sculpture hair salon next door, leaving Chloe trembling as she ran home. Eighteen-year-old Bryoni Goodwin told the *Croydon Advertiser*, 'He came in and said, "Have you seen my Tia Sharp?"' Hazell was wearing a white vest and baseball cap. When he came into the salon, he burst into tears. 'He went straight up to my boss and he was crying and swearing,' Bryoni recalled. 'He said, "Have you seen Tia? She's missing. I'm Tia's grandfather." He was swearing a lot but not at anyone. It was just there was a lot of bad language. Then he started saying that he that he did not want to find her in a forest, he wanted to find her in McDonald's eating a 99p burger. Then he was gone.'

At first, Bryoni didn't realise that the man was wanted

by the police but she then saw an appeal on the news and she, too, called 999.

Teams of officers began searching Cannon Hill Common in Morden. His childhood home, a terraced former council house, was nearby. The police had good reason to search there. A local man named only as Jamie, who was thought to have been at school with Hazell, said, 'I knew he would come back here. He lived next to the common with his father. He had a tough upbringing.'

A local man spotted him and dozens of police officers combed the area. Then, before nightfall, they got lucky and found him hiding in the woodland near the allotments. He had covered himself with a blanket and had hidden under a log but was pinpointed by a police helicopter using a thermal-imaging camera.

34-year-old onlooker Lisa Magnavacca, who lived opposite the scene of the arrest, said, 'A lady out walking her dog came across him. Apparently he was just huddled under a blanket in the woods. The dog disturbed him and the lady went straight to the police on the common. The police were here already. We saw seven or eight officers going into the wood and bringing him out.'

Word that Hazell was in the park had spread via social networking sites and BlackBerry Messenger. A crowd of locals gathered, who were soon baying for Hazell's blood. As a police helicopter hovered overhead, a dozen plain-clothes officers approached Hazell. He was arrested, handcuffed and dragged into a white police van that they had driven onto the common at 8.40pm. A witness said Hazell was 'completely drunk and out of it'.

As he was driven away, it took 50 officers to hold back

the group of young men and women who had gathered. They began shouting 'animal' and 'scum'. The van then drove off towards the main road where up to 100 people were gathered. They chased the van, screaming expletives as he was taken to nearby Sutton police station.

Twenty-two-year-old mother of one Chloe Hill, from Carshalton, Surrey, told the *Sunday Mirror* that people had rushed to the scene after hearing that Hazell had been spotted in a shop by eleven-year-old Chloe Bird. Some had keys clenched in their fists as weapons.

'It spread over Twitter and Facebook that the police were looking for him on the common,' Ms Hill said. 'So a big group went looking for him. Then they found him hiding in a bush. He looked really scared.'

'As the van got back on to the road, there was a lot of anger,' said Ms Magnavacca. 'People were shouting "scum" and kicking the van, running alongside it as it drove him up the road.'

Another onlooker said, 'He looked like he was crying.'

CHAPTER FIVE

FORENSICS

The forensic teams had moved into Tia's grand mother's house in New Addington to start work. They had the place to themselves. Hazell had gone on the run and been arrested. Christine Bicknell was not there either. She had been seen being driven away from the house that morning. Number 20 The Lindens was then cordoned off as white-suited forensic officers got to work.

The neighbours were in shock when they saw the forensic team move in. For some, it fulfilled fears that they had suppressed for the last seven days.

'I have just been told,' said 20-year-old resident Chloe Hickie. 'I feel sick… I didn't want to say it but I had a gut feeling because she hadn't been seen for a week. It makes me feel sick to my stomach. I am in absolute shock.'

The question on everyone's lips was: Why did it take the police so long to find the body? Tia's corpse was only found at 4pm on Friday, 10 August, more than a week since she had been reported missing. And it was not as if it had been found somewhere out in the woods, or in a skip, or in pieces in the local tip. The body was right there in the small terraced house where she had last been seen, in the house Hazell shared with Tia's grandmother Christine. The police, it had widely been reported, had searched the house several times before. They had even employed a sniffer dog.

Shaking her head in disbelief, 47-year-old Marcia Linton said, 'To think, she's been in that house all that time.'

At that point, though, it remained unclear whether the body had been in the house all the time since Tia's disappearance, or if it had been moved into the property some time later. Rumours were rife. Indeed, detectives were coming to believe that it had been moved several times during the week. They were examining the possibility that it had been switched between various lofts along the terrace to put investigators off the scent.

Once the police cordon went up, a crowd of some 150 New Addington residents gathered to express their displeasure. Some directed their anger at the police. Most said that they found it baffling that officers could have searched the house repeatedly and failed to find her body. . 'How on earth did the police go into the house and do a search and not find her?' asked 37-year-old Simone John, who lived in the next street. 'That's a real mess. If that had been a drugs offence, every single piece of that house would have been turned upside down. Things have been missed.'

For him, it was a plain dereliction of duty.

Another resident, 47-year-old Marcia Linton, said, 'To think she's been in that house and nobody knew. Where could she have been hidden? It's incredible. They even had a dog in there but it obviously didn't pick anything up.'

The residents of New Addington were voicing the thoughts of the whole country. How could the missing schoolgirl's body be in the house both the police and the family had been in and out of for nearly ten days? Tia's closest relatives had lived there, eaten and slept there during that time. The interview former detective Mark Williams-Thomas had carried out with Stuart Hazell and David Sharp, which the whole country had seen, was filmed there only metres from where Tia's body lay rotting.

Neighbours also found it hard to believe that Hazell had been interviewed by detectives as a witness only two days earlier and had not been arrested. There was little doubt in anyone's mind who the guilty party was. There was anger that Hazell had taken part in the candlelit procession wearing a white T-shirt appealing for the return of Tia. He was even said to have joined in the search before he suddenly went missing. And he appealed for her return on TV.

'Weren't you watching him?' one man shouted at the police. 'Why didn't you stop him?'

Detective Chief Superintendent Kevin Hurley, who had recently retired, attempted to explain: 'The police are so concerned about being criticised that they will not act promptly and robustly like they once did. So in this case, they would be concerned about getting it wrong and being seen to have acted insensitively in the face of the family and, therefore, their jobs would be at risk.'

But the press weren't to be satisfied with this this as a response to their concerns.

'Are the best people in the police – i.e. those best at hunting killers or catching robbers – necessarily promoted in a box-ticking culture that appears to value higher those who possess tact and sensitivity?' asked the *Daily Mail*.

Hurley admitted that officers had been at the house for a week and conducted a search of the property with a sniffer dog several days before. Although Natalie had then returned to Mitcham to look after her other two children, it was thought that she had slept overnight at the house where the body was found – which only made the situation more unsettling.

Commander Basu said that the body was only located after a full forensic search of the house was carried out. It was only when it was clear that the body had been found within the confines of the house, not outside in the garden or in any outbuilding, that Tia's mother Natalie was to be informed.

Another neighbour, 46-year-old mother of three Ginny Oteng, said, 'I have kids of my own the same age as Tia and I was worried because I thought there was a child snatcher out there. I was praying Tia would be found alive and well. I had my suspicions but it is still such a shock.'

Gavin Barwell, MP for the Croydon Central constituency that covers New Addington, asked for the public not to rush to condemn the police. He wrote on his blog, 'The police and forensic teams now have a serious job to do and I ask that we all please allow them to get on with trying to close a case which has, in such a short period of time, affected so many of us in Croydon and around the country. Despite the sad end to an emotional week, I want to praise the community in New Addington for their relentless dedication in trying to help their neighbour's family. So often in times of tragedy come inspirational displays of community.'

However, former Detective Chief Inspector Martyn Underhill was critical of the procedures the police employed. He told the *Independent*, 'The rule with a missing child is to clear the ground under your feet. You have to ask why it wasn't done earlier.'

Another senior policeman, retired Commander John O'Connor, said that it was 'unforgivable' for Scotland Yard to take a week to find Tia's body – and to let her suspected killer go on the run. He said that detectives should have ripped Tia's grandmother's house apart far sooner. The signs were all there. They should have done it directly after it came to light that the story Hazell had given the police did not match the one he had told his father.

'The police should have gone into that house quicker,' he told the *Sun*. 'Clearly Hazell should have been treated as a suspect from the off. He was the last person to see Tia alive. There were conflicting reports on what he said. If police have enough evidence to bring in sniffer dogs, they have enough evidence to pull the place apart. It's unforgivable they didn't do that. You can't rely on a dog – you need human brains. They haven't done very well. That child should have been found much quicker.'

Worse still, the Met had let their prime suspect slip through their fingers.

'How has Hazell managed to go on the run when he

should have been under surveillance?' O'Connor said. 'They didn't know if the child was alive or dead, so how was he able to slip away right under their noses?'

Former policemen were now slugging out in the press and retired Detective Chief Superintendent Kevin Hurley tried to explain the police process once again.

'Why has it taken so long to uncover the body?' he asked in the *Sun*. 'There may well be good tactical reasons in the way the police were going about their investigation and it may well have all been going to plan. But my concern is that I tend to see a lack of robustness and even nosiness developing among our police officers today. The reason for that is they will not take action until they are absolutely certain they are on robust and strong ground.'

He called for a return to old-fashioned policing. 'How can we create a situation where officers are prepared to be more nosy?' he said. 'When cops go round to speak to people, they often get a gut reaction, particularly detectives. When they are speaking to material witnesses, there was a time when, frankly, they'd have arrested them on the spot and brought them in. But there's real concern now about their own protection of their jobs, so they are less willing to perhaps do that these days.'

Reporters from the *Sun* discovered that some detectives involved in the investigation were not even aware that the interview with Hazell had appeared on ITV News the night before he was arrested, where he recalled his last conversation with Tia.

Later, senior officers said they noticed some telltale clues in the interview. For example, Hazell spoke of Tia in the past tense, indicating that he already knew she was dead. Former Detective Chief Superintendent Sue Hill told the *Sun*, 'I found the Hazell interview a bit odd, as he was talking about Tia in the past tense. He said, "I loved her."'

In her eyes, that should have made Hazell an immediate suspect – though perhaps it was a question of being wise after the event.

Hazell even described how he had cleared up the house that morning – and he had washed Tia's clothes. What had gone on in the house that night that it needed vacuuming? And why had her clothes needed cleaning? It could easily have been that he was trying to clear up any forensic evidence that might cause him a problem later.

The ex-Superintendent was also suspicious when Hazell said Tia had gone out without her mobile phone. 'Teenagers never leave home without their mobiles,' said Hill. In Tia's case, this was born out by testimony from the rest of the family.

Although the investigating officers seemed to overlook such telltale clues, Hill could understand why they had not searched the house earlier. 'You've got a corroborative witness who agreed with Hazell that Tia was seen leaving the house,' she said. 'You've got to go with the evidence and remember there is a grieving family there. Clearly the body was well hidden because the family have been there all week and so have the police.'

However, ex-detective Mark Williams-Thomas, the criminologist who interviewed Hazell for ITV News, was closer to the case and he said he was 'angry' that police had not conducted a thorough search of the house sooner. 'The first thing officers are asked on the missing-persons form is, "Has the house been searched?"' he said. 'It should have been searched thoroughly right away.'

While bedding had been removed in a small-scale search earlier in the investigation, the decision to rip the house apart was only made after a sniffer dog trained to detect dead bodies picked up the scent. More evidence had then been collected. A large holdall and 10 brown parcels marked as evidence had then been removed from the house. It was only then that a team of 40 forensic officers wearing hooded blue-and-white suits and shoe protectors moved in. Officers trained to detect blood, DNA and fibres smashed open wall cavities, floorboards and cupboards, and a ladder was employed to gain access to the roof area. Meanwhile, police had lined the narrow streets on the housing estate to keep the public at bay, sealing off the area with tape.

After the body had been found, Commander Neil Basu admitted that 'there will be a lot of questions' about the police inquiry. Indeed, a large-scale inquiry was instigated, although it did little to blunt the criticism of the Force at the time.

The Metropolitan Police faced further criticism after it emerged in the press that Angie Niles learned about her granddaughter's death from the television. She was watching Sky News when it was reported that a body had been found. Mrs Niles was later heard sobbing uncontrollably in her house in Mitcham.

One of her neighbours said, 'How sick. She's heard about her granddaughter's murder on the news.'

But Mrs Niles was not alone in her distress. Later she told the press that her son had taken the news badly.

'David is distraught,' she said. 'He was on the phone to me and couldn't even speak.'

News that a body had been found spread around the estate in minutes. Natalie Sabine, a friend of Tia's mother, said that she was still searching for Tia when she learned the news on her BlackBerry: 'There was a message over BBM. When I spoke to one of the family, he said they were all at the police station. He didn't say Stuart was there. It was just Christine and Stuart in the house last night.'

Mrs Sabine was also shocked that the police had not found the body earlier. 'I was in that house,' she said. 'I was there, I've been there six days. People went into the loft. I was in the cupboard under the stairs because I put the electric key in. We didn't know, of course we fucking didn't.'

She also received a text saying that Hazell had 'done a runner'. Appalled, she pulled off her 'Missing' T-shirt and a friend ripped it to pieces. Many of the friends and neighbours who had helped in the search were now close to hysteria.

CHAPTER SIX

TRIBUTES AND RECRIMINATIONS

Floral tributes from friends and well-wishers began arriving that night. Two laminated portraits of Tia were fixed to a garage wall. Lighted candles on the ground in front of them made up a makeshift shrine. More candles were placed around the nearby bus stop. This was strange.

'People were leaving candles at the bus stop. But it doesn't even look like she made it to the bus stop,' said neighbour 63-year-old Anthony Bramwell.

During the following day, a steady stream of neighbours and friends visited the home of Tia's grandmother at The Lindens, clutching flowers. Twenty-six-year-old photographer Billie-Jo Butler arrived with her three daughters. She was a friend of Tia's mum. 'I helped search for her,' she said. 'I handed out leaflets. I'm really stressed that it's happened here.'

They added the growing pile of condolence notes, flowers and teddies, and left in tears.

'This is so shocking for everyone around here,' she said.

A bouquet from Tia's mother carried a card that read, 'Rest in peace, Tia Sharp. My love is with the family, from Natalie.' Another card read, 'Tia, may your precious little soul now rest in peace. An angel we could have done with here on earth, spread your wings you're free to fly. With love from all who care. Addington's Angel.' And another, 'You are now with the angels and no more nasty people. You can rest in peace. We love you very much.'

Among the tributes were more touching messages.

'Rest in peace,' said one. 'Justice will be served.'

'Tia Sharp, beautiful angel, taken too soon, our thoughts are with all of you,' said another.

Forty-six-year-old Nicky Taylor and forty-year-old Shara Kinsley turned up to light two candles for Tia. 'She was only a child,' said Taylor. 'It's so sad.'

While tributes were being paid, there was a dramatic turn in the story that Sunday when the *Observer* announced that Christine Bicknell had also been arrested on suspicion of having helped her lover murder the missing 12-year-old. Then 39-year-old Paul Meehan, a neighbour, was arrested on suspicion of assisting an offender and held in custody. Meanwhile, as the murder inquiry broadened, more forensic teams could be seen on the estate, rummaging through wheelie bins and scouring grass verges in the search for fresh evidence.

The Metropolitan Police apologised for the 'stress and concern' caused by their delay in finding the body. But that did little to still the feelings that were running high on the estate.

'There's a mixture of anger and heartbreak,' said 44-year-old neighbour Dale Robertson. 'People feel aggrieved. They were duped. Even people who couldn't get out on the searches have posted up on Facebook that they are angry and that they were duped.'

Like other locals, Mr Robertson said thorough searches of the house should have been done sooner. 'I don't think it happened soon enough,' he said. 'After 24 hours they should have been ripping that house apart... People are angry and upset. They are still questioning why it has taken seven days. It's unbelievable. This time last summer there were 30 or 40 children here playing on the estate. Now most are too scared to come out.'

Fifty-six-year-old community care worker John Smithies blamed the authorities. 'Considering the police were searching through my bin, you would have thought they would have done a more thorough job the first time around,' he said. Then there was the expense. 'Extra police were drafted in, taken off the Olympics, which must have cost a lot. You would have thought they would first have searched the home.'

Forty-nine-year-old Elaine Alchin, who lived next door to the grandmother's house where the body was found, said, 'I cannot believe it. To think that she was in there all that time. But we knew something was wrong, that she might have actually never left the house, when CCTV of her when she was meant to have gone to Croydon never turned up... I'm so angry with the police because she could have been found a lot sooner. They just didn't search properly. Had they found her sooner, we'd be days ahead... now. It's such a shame.'

'It's absolutely disgusting,' said 61-year-old chartered accountant Joe Desouza, who was visiting the scene with his wife Malita. 'It makes you think that this girl could have been our grandchild. We cannot comprehend it.'

Former Scotland Yard detective Graham Sutton told BBC Radio 4's *Today* programme that the police investigation may have been hampered by senior officers' unwillingness to upset relatives in what began as a missing-person inquiry. 'That may mean the investigation is not as robust and thorough as it ought to be,' he said.

DCI Colin Sutton, who caught Milly Dowler's killer Levi Bellfield, said he was surprised at how long the police operation had taken. 'The first rule of a missing child inquiry is to search the home,' he said. 'I am desperately sad for the family and desperately angry the house wasn't cleared earlier.'

But some neighbours managed to find a positive side to the tragedy. Thirty-eight-year-old Sara Messenger, who works for a construction company, drew comfort from the way residents had rallied around to search for Tia. 'People have the wrong impression of the estate,' she said. 'The way everybody pulled together proves there is a strong community.'

This illustrated the tight-knit nature of the troubled estate. It seems that Tia's death had a silver lining, bringing out the best in local people. Suddenly, there was a community spirit where little had existed before.

In an attempt to explain the police failure to find the body, Commander Besu said, 'An initial visit was made on

3 August to assess the situation and examine the property.' However, he admitted mistakes were made during a second search, two days later. This exercise had taken two hours and the family had given their consent.

'All parts of the premises were searched,' he said, 'including the location where a body was discovered on Friday, 10 August.'

Initially, the police had been involved in the hunt for a missing person. By 5 August they believed that Tia was dead and were looking for a body. Nevertheless, Commander Besu was not entirely happy with everything that had taken place.

'An early review has been conducted and it is now clear that human error delayed the discovery of the body within the house,' he said. 'We have apologised to Tia's mother that our procedures did not lead to the discovery of the body on this search.'

The police had visited the house again on Wednesday, 8 August.

'This was not a search,' said Commander Besu. 'But the attendance of a body-recovery dog was to assist the investigation team in their inquiries. It is not appropriate to comment further on aspects of the criminal investigation currently being conducted but our investigation was such that it was decided that a further intrusive search needed to be undertaken – it was that search which resulted in the discovery. On behalf of the Metropolitan Police, I apologise for the distress and concern this delay will have caused. A continuing review and examination of our search processes will be undertaken to ensure such a failing is not repeated.'

But this explanation did not satisfy local people. One neighbour was outraged by the ineptitude of the authorities: 'The apology is fine but it's too little, too late,' she said. 'The police know they have cocked up. It is the senior bosses who need to come under fire for this, not the officers here. They've been fantastic.'

The press were critical too and it was not thought that the critical examination of the case would end there. Already it was being said that a criminal justice review would be launched, examining how agencies and police supervised Tia's family during the investigation. Indeed, the police investigation was facing intense scrutiny, both through an inquiry led by the Independent Police Complaints Commission and also by the Inspectorate of Constabulary.

The probation officers' and family court staff union, Napo (formerly National Association of Probations Officers), also said it believed that a series of reviews would be launched into issues relating to Tia Sharp's disappearance and death. The London Borough of Croydon's safeguarding board was expected to open inquiry into what involvement the murdered schoolgirl had had with social services in the months before she died.

Siobhain McDonagh, the MP for Mitcham, was not slow to call for an investigation into what went wrong. 'There is an immediate need to find out who was responsible for the murder,' she said. 'After that, we need to find out what police and everybody else could have done differently.'

Leader of Croydon Council, Mike Fisher, appealed for calm to allow the police to carry on their investigation.

After that he thanked the local volunteers who had helped the police in their week-long search for Tia.

'Our thoughts and sympathy are with Tia's family and friends at this incredibly difficult time,' he said. 'The last week has been extremely traumatic for everyone involved and the outcome of events is a deep tragedy for all of us. I do, however, want to say a personal thank you to everyone from the community who rallied round to help in the search. Their efforts and compassion are to be commended and I would now urge people to remain calm as the priority has to be for the police to be allowed to continue their investigations.'

But this did not still criticism in the press. The most blistering attack on the police came from the *People*, who said,

> The first rule of any missing child inquiry is for police to search the family home. Thoroughly.
>
> So why didn't officers who'd launched a nationwide hunt for 12-year-old Tia Sharp do that? What excuse – apart from stupidity and incompetence – can there possibly be for an army of detectives to miss a dead child's body in a three-bedroom council house? And how come they had to bring in a sniffer dog trained in decomposition to find Tia? By the time they discovered her, she had lain dead for up to eight long, hot days. Don't coppers have noses? Aren't THEY trained to smell decomposition?

The paper went on to give the reason as 'politically correct policing', adding, 'This was about officers terrified of doing their job properly for fear of infringing the family's human rights, for fear of being called "insensitive", for fear of being disciplined, prosecuted, even sacked. This was a hunt conducted to suit what police chiefs clearly feel is THE most important thing these days – public opinion and keeping their jobs.

'No one knows how Tia Sharp died yet but, if there was half a chance she was alive, they should have taken that house apart.

'That's their job and if anyone prevented them from doing it, that person needs to be fired.

'Because they let Tia Sharp down very badly!'

According to the *People*, the police did look in the exact spot where the corpse, believed to have been wrapped in Tia's grandmother's rug, was found – but missed it completely.

When she heard that Christine had been arrested, Tia's great-aunt, 43-year-old Karen Walker, said, 'I can't believe Christine had anything to do with her death. It's not the Christine I know.'

Tia's real granddad, Paul Sharp, however, said he felt sick after he heard the news. He was by now adamant that Christine was in the wrong for getting together with Hazell, whom she knew had previously dated Natalie. 'I don't ever want to speak to her and I don't even want to speak to my daughter,' he said. 'They have let that man back into their lives. Natalie got rid of him once and then Christine let him back in again. It's disgusting and I don't want to know.'

According to Paul Sharp, Hazell had been homeless, living on the street, and they took pity on him. He was also angry that his ex-wife was again using his name: 'Her real name is Bicknell,' he said. 'That's what she's been using since our divorce.'

When he'd learned of Tia's death, Paul Sharp had promised he would do everything in his power to make sure the killer paid. 'Whoever has done this to my granddaughter will pay, no doubt in my mind,' he said. 'Until I find out exactly what's happened, I'm not feeling for anybody. All I feel for is Tia. I have made a promise to her that I will not leave it until justice is done.'

His went on to say his granddaughter would be a candle in his heart until he died. 'I don't need to light a candle. The only time I lit a candle was to show her the way home in the darkness.' She was, he said, a 'beautiful, happy girl'.

'I hope her killer dies in jail,' he added.

Paul Sharp and his son David were to have taken Tia away on a caravan holiday that week along with Paul's daughter Danielle from another relationship, who was also 12. 'Now that's all gone and I'm destroyed,' Paul told the *Sun*.

Paul had come from his home in Newcastle to help in the search for Tia when he heard from his son on Saturday that she was missing. 'I was in shock,' said Paul. 'I said, "What do you mean, she is missing?" He said the police had been informed and he [David] would keep me up to date. He was in bits.'

But when he heard that her body had been found, Paul took Danielle to a friend's in Bognor Regis. 'I had to cuddle my 12-year-old, who was crying in my arms,' he said. 'It's horrible, terrible.' The two girls had been very close. 'Danielle grew up with Tia until she was six. It's killing me, all this. My daughter has been crying all night. This morning she won't get out of bed, she's cuddling her pillow. It's awful.'

Paul described how Tia and Danielle were the 'best of pals': 'They used to love playing cooking games together,' he said. 'Tia had this plastic cooker and was always making pretend tea and cakes and serving them to you.'

Tia's other grandfather, 52-year-old Stephen Carter, left flowers and a card at the growing shrine outside the house where they body had been found. The card said, 'To my darling granddaughter, sleep peacefully my angel. Until we meet in heaven, lots of love granddad (Steve).'

But Mr Carter was also determined that justice would be done. 'We will have our day in court,' he vowed. 'There will be justice for my granddaughter.'

A group of young mothers were also visiting the makeshift shrine. 'We didn't know her but wanted to pay our respects,' said one of them. 'I've got young children. I just can't imagine what that family is going through.'

Tia's loss had hit her mother Natalie and step-father David Niles hard but they were putting a brave face on it. They were 'in denial', relatives said. David's mother, Angie Niles, spoke to the press.

'It broke my heart to see him,' she said. 'He is in complete denial. I told him, "David, you have to face the facts now. You've got to open your eyes." But he can't. He still doesn't believe that it's Tia's body. He said to me, "Mum, we just don't know."'

The post-mortem and inquest had not yet been completed.

Two police officers were on duty outside the couple's Mitcham home. One officer was posted outside the second-floor flat; the other stood on the ground floor and told well-wishers that Ms Sharp and Mr Niles were not at the address. However, flowers and cards were left outside that building as a tribute to Tia. One message read, 'You are one of the brightest girls ever and you will be a bright star in the sky for ever.'

'It's not just grief,' said Mrs Niles. 'He is in a state of complete shock. I asked him about the arrests but he just doesn't want to believe it.'

She, too, was affected. 'I am deeply shocked and I am going to miss that little girl so much,' she said. 'It is just so tragic.'

Tributes to Tia were also displayed outside Raynes Park High School in Merton, which Tia had attended. One note there read, 'We will miss you so much. School will never be the same without you.' The school opened its doors despite the summer holidays and hundreds of students and parents signed a book of condolence and bought flowers. But somehow the death of Tia had still not sunk in. The depths of the tragedy were yet to be plumbed.

CHAPTER SEVEN

VISITING THE SHRINE

Despite the difficulty of coming to terms with their loss, on 12 August Natalie Sharp and David Niles summoned up courage and visited the shrine set up for Tia near the house in New Addington, where the residents had left candles, flowers, teddy bears, a photograph of the youngster and a poem that described her as 'heaven's little angel'. With her head in her hands, Natalie broke down. Weeping uncontrollably, she had to be supported by her partner David. They placed an orchid and a soft toy on the makeshift shrine, just yards from her mother's home. Along with the flowers they left on the pavement was a note that read, 'Our baby girl, We love you very much and always will. Sorry baby this neva [sic] should have happened. I wish I was there to protect you. We know you're safe now and you're at home with us everywhere we go.' It was signed 'Love Mum, Dad, Jack and Harry. XXX'

After spending five minutes at the scene, Natalie Sharp became so overwhelmed with grief that David Niles and another family friend had to carry her back to the police minibus that had brought them.

Steven Carter also visited the scene to lay a yellow rose with a pair of purple angel wings attached and a noted saying, 'My darling baby girl Tia. Daddy loves you dearly. I want you to stay safe in the arms of the angels. Love always. Daddy.'

Accompanied by his father, brother and three female friends, Carter wiped away his tears as he spoke of the anguish about the delay in the discovery of the body. 'It has hit us all very hard,' he said. 'In my wildest thoughts I didn't think it would end like this. I am devastated. I will never get to see my little girl again. I will never be able to hold her and kiss her.'

He wept as he asked, 'Why did this happen?'

Hugging his son, his father replied, 'There is no reason. She never harmed anybody, son. No child deserves this, especially my granddaughter.'

Tia's dad then revealed that, when he had first arrived the house in New Addington the previous Saturday, he had been refused entry by Hazell. 'I stayed outside the house and they wouldn't let me in,' he said. 'And Stuart Hazell walked over and put his hand on my shoulder and looked me in the eye.'

He had told the father of the missing child to 'be strong'.

'That now feels horrible,' said Carter. 'Now it seems so much harder because, when I was outside that house, I was probably only feet away from her body, and to know that is heartbreaking. If I had known then what I know now, I would have gone into the house and searched it myself.

'I know the police have done their job and I'm grateful but I think they could have investigated that house more from the start.'

He also spoke of his heartache and recalled the last time he saw his daughter: 'She jumped into my arms and told me she loved me. We spoke about her school, what she was doing... she called me Daddy. I'll miss her for ever.'

He said he felt 'heartbroken, angry, robbed of my beautiful little girl', adding, 'I want justice for my daughter – the proper way. All I keep doing is crying and praying for vengeance. My little girl will never get to her 16th, 18th or 21st birthday. We have been made to suffer. I'm so upset and angry. I'm feeling pain while everyone else is grieving.'

Also on hand was Tia's aunt Maxine Carter, who said, 'It's the worst living nightmare ever. It doesn't end – we are hurting so bad inside.'

The bouquets and hand-written notes piling up on the estate were also having a powerful effect on the residents.

'Just going down to look at all the flowers brings tears to your eyes,' said one of Christine Bicknell's neighbours, Joanne Hickmott.

Fifty-two-year-old Janette Dixon, who left a teddy bear at the memorial, said, 'It's heartbreaking. I have got four grandchildren of my own and the idea that something like this could happen is just devastating. The whole community was out searching for her, all day and every day, but she was in that house all the time. It is unbelievable.'

The family of Christine's neighbour Paul Meehan, who

as already mentioned had also been arrested, were baffled at the police's interest in him, although he had been seen talking to news crews after Tia's body had been found and taking a very active interest in the search. 'I have two young children aged eight and twelve – it's very scary for them,' he had said.

His 35-year-old wife Bobbie refused to speak to the press and sought refuge in her parents' home in New Addington. But his 60-year-old mother Gaynor, who lives in Swansea with her husband Peter, said, 'We just don't know what has happened. The first we knew of it was when it came up on the news. We haven't been told any-thing else.'

However, Meehan was arrested and placed under investigation while his account of the events was thoroughly examined. The suspicion was that he had allegedly given a false account to the police in order to back up Hazell's version of the story.

While police officers awaited formal identification of the body found at Christine Bicknell's house in The Lindens, in the early hours of the morning of Monday, 13 August, Hazell was formally charged with Tia's murder. By then dozens of death threats had been posted online. And when Christine Bicknell was released on bail, she was advised not to return home, even though she had not been charged.

Paul Meehan was also released on bail, pending further inquiries. He had not been charged at this point either and he, too, was warned not to go back to the estate.

30-year-old resident Jason Moore was reported to have said, 'You've seen how much people care about this. You could see a lynch mob if any of them come back.' Another neighbour, too, said, 'I'd stay away. Everyone knows each other here. That's why it's been so shocking.'

There were fears for Hazell's safety too. The police said that Hazell would make his appearance in nearby Camberwell Green Magistrates' Court by video link as he risked being attacked by a bloodthirsty mob if he appeared in person. Even members of Tia's family were speaking openly of 'avenging' her death.

More details about the failure of the police search were also leaking out. It seemed that, after the police had conducted an initial full search of the house, they made a second sweep using dogs trained to detect dead bodies. This took two hours. Some detectives suspected the body was behind a door connecting the loft to that of an adjacent property. However, they did not check the neighbouring loft space because that would have required a search warrant.

Then, when a further search of Christine Bicknell's house was made on the Friday following the disappearance, a junior officer had insisted a sniffer dog was 'indicating' towards a bedroom ceiling. The officers themselves had also recognised the odour of decomposition. A senior officer co-ordinating the search initially insisted that the loft had already been checked but then was persuaded to change his mind. When detectives lifted the loft hatch, they saw what they described as a large 'container', possibly a rigid suitcase. This contained Tia's body but it was only big enough to house her torso, so her arms and legs were sprawled outside, it was said.

An internal review was then launched to discover why

earlier searches had failed. The delay of a week before Tia's body was recovered meant there had been significant decomposition and, as the post-mortem examination was halted on Saturday, there were fears that it might not be possible to ascertain the cause of death. One police source told *The Times*, 'There is no question you can ask that we aren't asking ourselves. We get it.'

Recently retired Metropolitan Police superintendent Malcolm Baker, a former search specialist, raised more concerns. He said that it was 'very worrying' that a force that used to have the best search teams in the country had made such an error. He could not understand why the search that missed the body was conducted in the early hours of the morning.

'I am very worried about what happened in New Addington,' said Mr Baker. 'Searching at night is never a good idea unless absolutely necessary. To search properly, you need to look under floorboards, lift carpets, send a dog into the roof space – I have to ask, was all that done in a couple of hours in the middle of the night? The potential impact on the case is significant. Allowing the body to decompose can make it much harder to get a cause of death from the post-mortem, which, in turn, makes it potentially harder to prove murder.'

Mr Baker said that he was concerned that, for a number of years, search skills had been downgraded and that the process would accelerate with police budget cuts. 'We spent a long time developing the specialist search capability in the Met,' he said. 'But in 2008 searching was transferred from an investigative command into a Protective Security Command.'

This was more than a merely bureaucratic change, he insisted. 'It stopped being at the heart of the investigative units and I watched it go downhill from there – it became more about cost, rather than supporting and adding value to investigations.'

On Monday, 13 August 2012, Hazell made an appearance in court via video link from Sutton Police Station. He was dressed in a blue T-shirt with an illegible slogan across the front and sat alone at a desk with a policewoman standing behind him. His voice cracked with emotion when he was asked to confirm his address: '20 The Lindens, New Addington, south London' – the very place where Tia had been found dead. He also confirmed his date of birth.

In a tense three-minute hearing, he was accused of murdering Tia Sharp between 2 August, the day before she was first reported missing, and 11 August, the day before he was finally charged. Asked whether he understood the charge against him, he replied simply, 'Yes, I do.'

Appearing on screen at Camberwell Green Magistrates' Court, he looked down at his hands and fidgeted with some paperwork on the table as he answered.

No plea was entered. A preliminary court hearing was scheduled for 19 November. Hazell was told that the court did not have the power to hear a bail application, which would have to be made before a senior judge at the Old Bailey. Until then, he was to remain in custody, isolated from other prisoners in Belmarsh for his own safety. He was also to appear by video link at the Old Bailey the following day, when he would be able to make an application for bail. Chairman of the bench Charu Joglekar said it was 'not appropriate' for prosecutor Mary Atere to give a short outline of the case because the court did not have jurisdiction for the matter.

However, more was forthcoming from outside the court, where a legal source revealed that police believed Tia was suffocated before her body was hidden in her grandmother's loft. It was said that Tia's remains were found wrapped in a black bed sheet and that she had been stuffed inside a plastic bin bag. Poignantly, the body had been found in the very house in which Tia had been born – Steven Carter and Tia's mother Natalie had lived there with grandmother Christine for more than a year before the relationship broke down.

Police forensic teams were still carrying out DNA tests on items recovered from the house and no official cause of death had been given after the post-mortem was halted. However, it was revealed that, apart from bruising, pathologists had not found obvious injuries on her body. This prompted the theory that she had either been smothered or strangled.

No relatives appeared in court. However, Angie Niles was on hand to speak for the family. 'You always think things like this happen to someone else,' she said. 'You see stories about James Bulger and others and you think it must be awful what the family are feeling. But you switch the telly off and forget about it because it is not actually happening to you. We are all in absolute shock and devastated. It is just awful, I can't find the words to describe how terrible this is.'

The shock of Hazell's arrest was still sinking in.

'It is all a bit surreal at the moment,' said Mrs Niles, 'as if we are on the outside looking in. But I think everyone is going to be up in the air until we know the whos, whys and the wherefores.'

She had only had a slight acquaintance with the defendant. 'I don't know Stuart Hazell,' she said. 'We talked a bit, hello and that. But I think I only saw him a couple of times. I didn't really see or hear much about him or Natalie's mum.'

Natalie, her son David and their two boys were still struggling to come to terms with the tragedy, she said. 'I speak on the phone to David every day a couple of times,' she said. 'I've told him not to worry about me, because I have bad health, but to concentrate on Natalie and the boys. He has got to be strong for them. But obviously he is devastated. David was in complete denial that it was even Tia's body right up until Sunday. I am just so glad all of his childhood friends have come out to support him. They have also been here to see me. The community has really come together.'

But the family had not yet talked about the tragedy. 'It is so raw [that] we haven't been able to sit down and talk as a family. We could end up making so many judgements and they might be wrong so, until we know, we don't want to speculate.'

Nor could she comment on Natalie's relationship with her mother Christine since the arrest. 'I don't think I can comment on that, to be quite honest,' she told the *Sun*. 'It is going to be so raw for Natalie.'

However, she was openly critical of the police. 'They came here and saw me the Saturday after Tia disappeared,' she said. 'They said, "We will keep in touch, we will keep you in the loop." Then it wasn't until this Saturday night when they came to see me and they said they would send a family-liaison officer round. But I haven't heard anything or seen anyone. We need support. I want David to support Natalie – she is in shreds, or bits, or however you like to put it.'

CHAPTER EIGHT

COURT APPEARANCE

That Wednesday, 15 August 2012, Stuart Hazell appeared at the Old Bailey via video link from Belmarsh prison. He sat next to a prison officer from Belmarsh as the judge, Mr Justice Saunders, opened the hearing.

Wearing an orange T-shirt and tracksuit bottoms, Hazell spoke only to confirm his name and that he could hear the proceedings. He remained seated throughout the 10-minute hearing, leaning forward to listen to the prosecutor Julian Evans as he outlined the case.

Represented by Lord Alex Carlile QC, Hazell made no application for bail. A provision date for the trial was set for 21 January 2013, although he would appear again at the Old Bailey before then on 19 November. When the judge brought the proceedings to a close, Hazell said, 'Thank you, sir.'

The trial was scheduled to last three weeks.

'We've no idea what the issues will be until we have evidence,' said Lord Carlile. 'It's possible there will be a lot of background, some of it from the family.'

According to the *Sun*, Tia's family were outraged that Hazell had been spared having to face court in the flesh a second time. They believed that he should have been brought into the courtroom in person to face his accusers and that he was being given special treatment.

'People want to see justice being done properly,' said family spokesperson Angie Niles. 'He'll be tried by the public in the end; they can't hide him for ever.'

For the moment, though, he was being shielded from the public.

'We're having to put on this brave face but Hazell hasn't had to show his,' she said.

It was thought that Hazell was being allowed to make these short remand appearances to save money, given the additional security that would have been required to protect him. Harry Fletcher of trade union Napo, which represents family court staff, said, 'In the circumstances, it would not have been deemed worthwhile to have taken him in.'

At that point, Hazell was on a 24-hour watch in high-security Belmarsh prison after receiving death threats from other prisoners. He was being kept in isolation on a wing housing paedophiles and rapists.

'Everyone in the kitchen was talking about him arriving,' a visitor to the Category A prison in south-east London told *The Sun*. 'Inmates are talking of death threats. You can hear his name being shouted out from cells. He's being kept in isolation and under 24-hour watch for his own safety.'

Meanwhile, Merton Council was setting up a case review into Tia's death. This was 'standard procedure', it was said.

'Our thoughts and condolences go out to all those who knew Tia,' said Chief Executive Ged Curran. 'The local Safeguarding Children Board will now commission a serious case review, the standard procedure in a tragic case such as this. The review will be assisted by the police, health services and local authorities.'

Serious case reviews are carried out when a child has died. It looks into the role played by local agencies in the life of that child and their family, and would aim to find out if any lessons could be learned about ensuring children's safety. Government guidelines say, 'The prime purpose of a serious case review is for agencies and individuals to learn lessons to improve the way in which they work, both individually and collectively, to safeguard and promote the welfare of children.'

Social services had, it emerged, been involved with the family on a number of occasions in the past. However, each time the authorities were happy that no further action needed to be taken with regards to the family, and each time the case was closed. It seemed that the last time the local authority took an interest in the family was in 2011, and there had been no contact between the authorities and the family since then.

'Questions need to be asked as to why social services did not act on the warnings,' one source told the *Sunday Mirror*. 'Tia was spending more time at her gran's and, ultimately, that was where her body was found. The review will investigate whether they did enough to protect her. It seems inexplicable nothing was done.'

Harry Fletcher of Napo said, 'Every month social services receives thousands of pieces of information... investigations only take place when it's reported a child is at risk.'

On Thursday, 16 August an inquest was opened at south London's Coroner's Court. In a five-minute hearing, it formally identified the body found in the loft of Christine Bicknell's house in New Addington as that of Tia Sharp. Detective Sergeant Eric Sword of the Metropolitan Police's Specialist Crime and Operations unit based at Sutton told the inquest that a post–mortem examination was still being carried out by a pathologist.

Asked by Coroner Roy Palmer if the body has now been formally identified, Mr Sword said, 'From the checks that we have been able to carry out, yes.'

'And that body is that of Tia Sharp?' the coroner asked.

'That is correct,' he replied.

Tia had had to be identified by her teeth, as her body was so badly decomposed after a week in the loft at her grandmother's house. The heat under the roof in the attic that August had speeded up decomposition, leaving the 12-year-old unrecognisable.

The cause of death remained a mystery. Forensic examination of the 12-year-old's internal organs and tissue drew a blank and detectives feared that they might never know exactly how Tia died, although they still suspected that she had been smothered.

'Without a cause of death, it makes the prosecution's job

incredibly difficult,' said Julian Young, a London solicitor advocate – equivalent to a barrister – who had represented in criminal cases for 35 years, including more than 200 homicide cases. 'If you are charged with murder, it means that X kills the victim unlawfully, not accidentally, therefore you have to be able to prove how that person died. The prosecution has to provide how the victim died and who did it and, if the pathologist comes back and says, "We can't find cause of death," the Crown has got really serious problems. It is as simple as that. They have got to prove something unlawful has been done,' he told the *Croydon Advertiser*.

Dr Stuart Hamilton, who had conducted more than 2,500 post-mortems since 2003, said the discovery of Tia's body after 7 days rather than 2 may have led to the failure to find a cause of death. 'The simple answer is… absolutely, this will have had an effect,' he said. 'The fresher a body is when we get it, the more we can say. Similarly, the longer someone lies undiscovered, the more the post-mortem changes and decomposition sets in. Also, if you are talking about a body that has been kept in a loft, then it is not going to have been kept in the optimum temperature, so decomposition will be much quicker, making it, again, more difficult to look for injuries or bruises.

'If you have a simple cause of death, like a gunshot wound, then something like that is usually going to be fairly apparent, even a long time after death. But if you have a more subtle cause of death, like a smothering, it can be difficult in a fresh body and very, very difficult with any degree of decomposition. Someone who has been lying around for a week is not going to be in a good condition.'

Once the post-mortem examination was completed, Stuart Hazell had the right to request a second one by a pathologist of his choice. Dr Palmer, the coroner, asked that this be carried out as soon as possible, so that Tia's body could be released to her family. The inquest was then adjourned.

After the hearing, MP Gavin Barwell criticised the police for 'clear mistakes' in their hunt for Tia's body but added that it wasn't the time for an inquiry into police conduct. Metropolitan Police Commissioner Bernard Hogan-Howe said he expected the investigation into the police errors to be completed within a few weeks. However, he thought that the failure to find Tia's body was not the fault of an individual officer.

'If we thought it was an individual human error, that would explain it,' he said. 'But we're carrying out a review because we're not happy that explains it. We've explained that it was human error but we want to go into it more. You can always blame the individual but we want to understand what processes and management decisions we've made that led to that failure. That's why we're carrying out a review and we hope in a few weeks' time we will have some conclusions from that, so that we make sure it doesn't happen again.'

The Independent Police Complaints Commission also said that it had received a number of complaints from residents but refused to launch an inquiry. An IPCC investigation would only be initiated if someone close to the case, such as a family member, claimed they were severely affected.

A police spokesman said the Met would not discuss

specific issues surrounding the case until the internal review was completed. The police were still hopeful a cause of death would be found. The spokesman cited the case of the singer Amy Winehouse as a high-profile example of how a cause of death could be established after an initial post-mortem had failed to find one.

Although there were still some tests outstanding, Tia's body was released to the defence in early September for them to conduct their own post-mortem.

Tia's grandmother Christine Bicknell had been keeping a low profile since Tia's body had been found and her lover Stuart Hazell had been arrested and charged. With an investigation as complex as this, nobody was beyond suspicion in the public eye, however unfair that may seem with regards Christine Bicknell's innocence. She had not returned to New Addington and had kept out of the limelight. However, news of her came from 41-year-old David Gawman, who used to be her lodger. Tia's body had been found above his old room. When he visited his old landlady, he told the *Sun* that she had hugged him. 'She then sobbed her heart out,' he continued. 'It's sickening to think we were all in that house waiting for news of Tia and her body was probably in the house all the time. I used to live a few feet from that loft. Natalie, Tia's mum, was in bits. We tried to keep her spirits up by having a laugh and a joke with her but she looked completely gaunt.'

Christine had been told to stay away. Even though it was reported that she doted on Tia, she was staying in a secret location and had apparently not been answering her phone. One friend was reported to have said, 'People have told her it's not a good idea to go to the funeral.'

Hannah Wilson of the *Croydon Advertiser* said, 'Stuart Hazell has done this interview [with ITV News] which raises suspicions and definitely made people question whether there are other members of the family that had some involvement or knew more than maybe we had been told at that stage.' In this case, Hannah and anyone else harbouring suspicions, was incorrect, but nevertheless the suspicions were there for a time.

'We were portrayed as the horrible ones,' said Christine in the documentary 'Living with a Killer'. 'We were the ones who had allowed it to happen. We were the ones who lured her there and allowed him… whatever… I don't know.'

The murder attracted some sick attention; a hoaxer, for example, claiming to be the chairman of Crystal Palace Football Club, told Tia's grandfather that there was going to be a tribute to her before the kick-off at Selhurst Park on Saturday, 18 August. Meanwhile, Natalie Sharp and David Niles moved out of their flat in Mitcham to escape unwanted attention.

It then appeared that a 'sick' Internet troll had begun impersonating the grieving Natalie on Facebook. The page, entitled 'RIP Tia Sharp RIP Little Angel' was created on 10 August, the day the schoolgirl's body was found. But when the tribute site was first set up, it spelled the young girl's name wrong, calling her Tia Sharpe instead of Sharp.

The first message read, 'R.I.P. my darling daughter I love you so much and I carnt [sic] believe you gone.' The following day, the troll attacked those who wanted to be involved in running the page. They wrote, 'I'm sorry everyone who wants to be admin. Came on and 119 (people) wanted to be admin. I'm sorry but it isn't happening she was my daughter not yours.'

That day, a post read, 'I'm not Tia's mother and I never will be but I was a very close family friend of Tia and her family and it is a very hard shock for me.'

The admission sparked outrage from all those involved who thought they were supporting a genuine tribute page. Supporter Tracy Murray commented, 'A little girl's family are grieving at this very minute over the loss of Tia and you think its right to put posts up saying you're the girl's mother? I bet you have never met the family in your life but [are] enjoying the attention. You sad lowlife have some respect for that family.' Another supporter, Nicola Emery, added, 'This is sick a poor little girl has been murdered and you, a sick human being, set up a page saying you are her mum. Why would you do that? Let Tia R.I.P. and stop playing horrible games. You're sick and twisted.'

No messages were left on the page after 11 August but the site was accessible for at least another two weeks until the *New Addington Advertiser* reported the page to Facebook in a bid to have its contents taken down.

The deception angered Tia's father Steven Carter, who told the *Advertiser*, 'I don't know what their game was. It doesn't help the family at a time when we are still all very upset and confused. I wasn't aware anyone had done this but I have only been looking at people's pages who I have accepted on Facebook and who I know.'

CHAPTER NINE

FUNERAL AND MEMORIALS

By 11 September government pathologists had given up trying to identify the cause of death. The release of Tia's body had also been delayed by the counsel for Stuart Hazell, who had asked for a re-examination.

Two post-mortems had failed to find the cause of death and, finally, the body was handed over to the family.

On 14 September, mourners dressed in black and pink lined the streets of south London to pay their respects as Tia's funeral procession made its way into north-east Surrey Crematorium in Morden. The family had asked onlookers as well as friends and family to dress that way.

'It is Natalie's arrangements and she has asked we come dressed in black and pink,' said Steven Carter. 'It was so strange to be out on the weekend shopping for her funeral, buying a new suit and pink tie.'

Pink balloons were tied to railings and fences in the streets around the cemetery as a tribute to Tia. The horse-drawn hearse was filled with flowers and the horses wore pink plumes. Her white coffin was adorned with a pink feather boa, hearts, butterflies and flowers spelling out the words 'Tia', 'Little Princess' and 'Little Angel'. Inside the coffin little Tia was also dressed in pink, one of her favourite colours. On top were wreaths that spelled out 'Our Girl' and 'Sister'.

The cortège was made up of at least 30 vehicles and included 3 trucks full of floral tributes shaped like stars and horses' heads. The truck displayed a mock-up of a BlackBerry mobile phone with a photograph of the 12-year-old's face in place of the screen. The procession included a fluorescent pink stretch Hummer with blacked-out windows.

The hearse was closely followed a car carrying Tia's mother Natalie, David Niles, her uncle David Sharp and, despite the warnings urging her not to attend, grandmother Christine Bicknell. Then came cars carrying other relatives and friends.

Some people threw flowers at the procession and the crowds that had gathered fell silent out of respect as it passed. Many wept at the sight of the small coffin. Balloons and banners lined the route. They festooned balconies, garden gates, trees and fences all the way to the 12-year-old's final resting place.

'I think she would be sitting there very proud, right now, of everyone,' said Steven Carter. 'I think she just touched everybody's hearts; even people who didn't know her were turning up to pay their respects. And even those who didn't know her fell in love with her. That much was clear today.'

As the procession passed by Tia's school, the silence was broken by intermittent sobs from the 800 pupils who had turned out to bid their schoolmate farewell. Many were visibly moved and had to be comforted in their grief by their families and teachers. Parents and school staff also had tears in their eyes. They bowed their heads as the cortège drove by.

In keeping with the occasion's pink-and-black theme, students wore pink clips, hair bands and scarves. And there were cerise pink dresses, jackets and ties, pink sashes, pink buttonholes, pink T-shirts with Tia's picture on the front, and babies with pink dummies, and some onlookers were holding pink roses. The children had left dedications in a garden on the school grounds.

One of the mothers of Tia's classmates was asked what the most fitting tribute could have been for the young girl. She replied, 'Words can't say more than what you have seen here.'

Children had also tied pink balloons on to the railings of a bridge that the cortège passed over on its way to the crematorium and the gates of the crematorium were decorated with more pink balloons and ribbons.

There were some 20 girls at the funeral that had been friends of Tia's. One was Eileen Smythe's daughter who had made pillowcases for Tia emblazoned with the message 'time to say goodbye'. These were hung on the railings of Grand Avenue, a few hundred yards from the crematorium where more then 500 relatives, friends and neighbours turned out to bid Tia farewell.

'Tia was a lovely girl. She was an angel, she was a very popular, independent girl,' said Ms Smythe. 'To Tia, pink was her best colour, her schoolbag was pink, so everyone's wearing pink.'

Another friend, 12-year-old Bethany, who used to get the same bus home, said, 'She was a really nice, pretty girl. We had loads of jokes together. It was very upsetting, just remembering all the good things that happened when she was around.'

Bethany's family had heard that Tia had gone missing when they were on holiday and learned of her death while travelling home. 'We were on our way home from holiday and cried all the way home,' said Bethany's 33-year-old mother Melaney. 'We turned up in the school and crematorium to pay respects to Tia.'

Forty-five-year-old Amanda Allen, who had twin boys at the school, also came to pay her respects, although she did not know Tia. 'I never ever met Tia,' she said, 'but, although I didn't, I don't feel it matters. I mean, she just touched everybody's hearts. It's all that has been talked about at the school for the last few weeks and I wanted to come down here and show my support. Everybody has been touched by it all.'

At the New Horizon Community Centre in Pollards Hill, where the 12-year-old took dance lessons, a book of condolence had been opened a day after her body was found on 10 August and, on the Friday of the funeral, many people brought candles and flowers to the centre. It was close to where Tia lived. 'She was a nice kid,' said Andy Hodge, who managed the centre. 'It's sad that it takes something like that to bring a community together.'

Christine Bicknell, nevertheless, was at the funeral and she took her place alongside Natalie, Steven Carter, David

Niles and David Sharp. During the service she sat with the family. Once again the family displayed a remarkable solidarity. Christine wore a pink shirt, black jacket and dark glasses. Her nails were multi-coloured. Everyone made an effort to make the grim event as bright as possible.

The hundreds lining the streets had, like the schoolgirl's family, waited more than a month to finally lay the tragic girl to rest. 'It has been a horrible, horrible long time to lay her to rest,' said Steven Carter before the service. 'It is hard knowing there is no cause of death because we still have no answers… It is very hard to take in. It feels like I've been shot. The main feeling is probably anger but I know the process will go on through the funeral and trial and I must keep it together. I have been thinking back on the good times, watching her as she grew up. I still just can't get used to the idea I am never going to see Tia grow up. There are so many things I don't know – who her best friend was, her favourite colour, her favourite food.'

Hundreds of friends and relatives from across New Addington and Merton were packed into the private service at crematorium. There were heart-warming tributes from family members and two of Tia's teachers. That afternoon the mourners also came to know more about the girl whose tragic story touched the heart of the nation. Photographs of Tia were circulated, along with the order of service and heartfelt messages. These told how the youngster often put the needs of others ahead of her own.

'I used to see you every day on the bus,' read one. 'You always offered me your seat when I had my grandson with me. You are a beautiful girl, always so kind and thoughtful.'

Another said, 'Will always remember you after your

bubbly personality, your smile, your kindness and most of all the way you always did your hair and make-up.'

'Baby Cakes' by 3 Of A Kind played as the coffin entered the chapel. More of Tia's favourite songs were played during the service. These included Eric Clapton's 'Tears In Heaven', which he wrote after the death of his four-year-old son, 'Stay With Me' by Ironik, and 'All Things Bright and Beautiful'. The funeral ended with 'Low' by American rapper Flo Rida.

One family member told the congregation, 'Tia was a happy, helpful girl – and a real girly girl too. She loved nothing better than dressing up and prancing around in her pink clothes and doing her hair and make-up... Tia was taken from us far too soon in the worst possible way. But don't let anger eat away at you or your love for Tia.'

A teacher from her former primary school in Pollards Hill told how Tia was once sent out of class with a fellow pupil to make up following a dispute, only for her to come back in holding hands with the classmate.

'What the teachers said about her just summed her up,' said Steven Carter. 'It brought a smile to people's faces. She was lively, bubbly and fun, that's what people were saying about her.'

Another mourner said, 'Everyone respected the fact that this was an occasion to remember Tia and celebrate her life.'

However, the occasion proved too much for Natalie. Tia's mother was too distraught to deliver her own final farewell and her eulogy was read out by a member of the clergy.

Steven Carter said that, although the funeral brought some closure, 'We are still seeking justice.'

After the funeral, Natalie talked to the press for the first time. Though she had to avoid details of the case for legal reasons, she told the *Sun* of the suffering she had been through since Tia went missing. Throughout the search, she said, she had tried to keep her spirits up and continued to hope for the best. Then she described the moment she had heard that Tia's body had been found.

'It's like being twisted from the inside,' she said. 'It has been pure hell. You see yourself become that family everyone watches on the news. It's not supposed to happen to people like yourself, it's always someone else, isn't it? All those other cases you've seen, the most horrible stories. You never think one day that will be you. But then it was me – my Tia.'

After Tia had gone missing the family had gathered at Tia's grandmother's home in New Addington. Although they were just feet from where the corpse lay, they had clung on to the forlorn hope that she was still alive. 'We were holding on to hope that she would be OK,' Natalie continued. 'As the days passed, the range of emotions we went through was like nothing I can describe. You feel empty, like you're being twisted from the inside, all the way from your stomach to your throat. You can't eat, you can't sleep; it's horrible. I wouldn't wish it on my worst enemy. All we could do was wait. But the more you wait, the more you know in your heart of hearts that it's not going to happen. It's the last thing you think about when you go to bed and the first thing you think about when you wake. It's still that way.'

The family's ordeal had been exacerbated when sick pranksters began taunting them over the phone. Tia's uncle David Sharp had been out searching when a call came on his mobile. 'She'd been missing for around three days,' said David. 'They'd seen my mobile number on the T-shirts we wore for the TV appeals. They were saying, "We've got her and we'll tell you where and when you can have her." It was a sick joke. The police traced the call to Scotland. They found a couple of lads sitting around drunk, making prank calls.'

But they were not the only ones to torment the family.

'It wasn't the only time,' said Natalie. 'We had lots of false messages. There were people calling, saying they had seen her at a bus stop. Someone said they had spotted her asleep on a park bench. We had people running around everywhere chasing up messages. For people to be sitting there having fun at that time, it just makes you so angry.'

Natalie had been at a friend's house when the police brought the news that Tia's body had been found. 'They asked to speak to me,' said Natalie. 'They took me into the dining room of my friend's house and that was when they dropped the bombshell.'

The impact was immediate. She collapsed. 'I hit the floor and I remember looking up and all I could see was kids, everyone's kids. I hit the floor. And when I looked up, everybody was looking at me and it was… my eyes told me I was in a nightmare.'

She was told they had found 'just remains… and that was it, and then they left'.

'There were sorrowful eyes looking down at me. I felt sick. I was vomiting every time I thought about it. To know that she was there that whole time. You hate the police for missing her, you hate yourself for not finding her; you hate everyone who has been in the house, everyone who has been near the house. I hated everybody,' she said. 'Tia was the life and soul of the party,' Natalie recalled. 'She was so popular with everyone.'

But she did not want sympathy. 'I just never want another person to have to go through this,' she said.

Christine Bicknell also recalled the moment, in the documentary 'Living with a Monster', that she had been told that the body had been found: 'I didn't want to believe it,' she said. 'I don't know what I thought. You know, she was coming home. She was coming home.' Even then she did not suspect that her partner Stuart Hazell was a killer. When asked whether she suspected anyone, she had said no.

David Niles told the *Daily Mail* that, when the police broke the news, he could not comprehend what he was being told. 'I couldn't believe it when they told me,' he said. 'I refused to believe it. I wanted there to have been some mistake. We were praying they would tell us a body had been there for 30 odd years – we were desperate. I remember asking them, "Are you sure it's not a cat or a dog?"'

Although it had been more than five weeks since the world learned that Tia's body had been found, Natalie and her partner David had not told her two brothers, aged three and one, of their sister's death – although keeping it from them was proving difficult.

'It's hard to be normal – how can you?' said Natalie to the *Sun*. 'The boys have to be told. To be honest, I'm not quite sure how we're going to do it. One of them has already started to notice. He's called out to a few girls in the street, thinking it's Tia. The other day he picked up her favourite sweets in the shop. We had to ask the man behind the till to just hide them under the counter, so we didn't have to explain.'

'How do you tell a child that age?' said David Niles. 'What can you say?'

Commissioner Bernard Hogan-Howe apologised to Tia's mother for not finding her daughter sooner and told her that two officers had been disciplined for the failure.

Croydon Borough Council then announced that they intended to knock down the house where Tia was murdered – perhaps even the whole terrace. Distraught at living near the scene, neighbours had already been rehoused, and the houses on either side of Tia's grandmother's house had been boarded up.

'We just couldn't stay there,' said 34-year-old mother-of-two Romaine Richards, who used to live next door. The ordeal of unknowingly living inches away from Tia's decomposing body for a week was too much for her. She was rehoused with her daughters, aged 8 and 13, in Selsdon. 'When we found out her body was found in the house, we were in shock,' she said. 'We came back to the house to get things but we just couldn't stay there. I was in tears; I had to go to the doctors because I was so stressed about it. We were offered counselling, which my daughter still needs.'

They moved in with her cousin in New Addington for a month before being found somewhere permanent. 'I'm pleased the council moved us. My eight-year-old daughter is still very disturbed.' And Romaine herself suffers from the recollection. 'I smelled a smell in my daughter's room the day before they found Tia,' she said. 'It was an unusual smell I hadn't smelled before. It didn't really dawn on me at the time. It plays on my mind even now… I feel sorry for all the neighbours. I couldn't have coped if I'd stayed there.'

Although the homes either side of grandmother Christine Bicknell belonged to the council, the other four in the terrace were privately owned. This meant the council would have to offer to buy residents out if they wanted to redevelop the site. The council had said they might do this so that they could demolish the entire terrace. 'Nobody wants to live there and nobody should be expected to live there,' said a spokesman. 'The plan is to knock them down but that won't be done until after the court case is over.'

The council owned numbers 20 and 21, which had to be left standing until after the trial of Stuart Hazell in case the jury wanted to visit the properties. 'It is most likely that then one detached house would be put there,' the spokesman said. 'Nobody should be expected to live there.'

The MP for New Addington Gavin Barwell said it would be insensitive to force families to carry on living there if they wanted to move and called on the council to do everything possible to help the residents.

'The house is a constant reminder of the tragedy,' said a neighbour. 'People avoid going near and children go elsewhere to play. It is so difficult to forget the terrible events.'

Another neighbour who lived just two doors from where Tia was found said, 'It's affecting my children and they don't want to play out there anymore. It is very disturbing because it's really hard to come to terms with it. You are reminded of it every time you go out. Other people can forget but, for us, there is a constant reminder.'

But there is a time and a place for a reminder. On 10 November 2012, a commemorative plaque was put up and a rhododendron bush planted in the garden of the Alwyn Club in New Addington. The club is for ex-servicemen, many of whom were involved in the search for Tia. At the unveiling ceremony, the Reverend Dawn Williams led prayers. After a minute's silence, she said, 'We remember the fun-loving, vibrant and creative girl she was. We can't imagine the grief felt by those who love her.'

Club manager Mrs Eileen Clements said, 'The members did a collection. We wanted to do something with it. I said we should do a planting and have a plaque made. A few members knew the family and were walking around for Tia. It has been positive; everybody is pleased and can see where the pennies have gone.' It was decided not to put the club's name on the plaque as it was considered to be from everybody in New Addington.

Councillor Tony Pearson concluded by praising the community for coming together during the search for the schoolgirl. 'This is in recognition of a community that came together and stuck together,' he said. 'She will not be forgotten.'

Meanwhile, on 7 December, the police announced, in a brief and succinct statement, that Tia's grandmother had been cleared of any and all connection with her grand-daughter's death.

Tia's other grandmother, her step-grandmother Angie Niles – who Tia had affectionately called 'Nangie' – wrote an open letter to the dead girl on behalf of the family, which she showed to the *Sunday Mirror*, expressing what it would be like to spend Christmas without her.

'We would just like to tell you how much we miss you each and every day,' it said. 'The thoughts that run through our heads will never leave us. But we truly believe you are up there shining like a bright star looking over us all, especially your little brothers, Jack and Harry. I think God was running out of angels, and perhaps that is why he took you from us. God bless you Tia.'

Mrs Niles said she would spend Christmas alone, away from the rest of Tia's family, but she told the newspaper, 'Christmas will be so hard for all of us. We all have so many happy times with Tia in our minds from years gone by.'

Everywhere she looked there were little reminders of the child. 'I have a pair of small Christmas trees she picked for me two or three years ago,' she said. 'She made me buy them because they were pink and that was her favourite colour. I've put them up and, even though I'm sad to look at them, they make me smile because she loved them.'

In the run-up to Christmas, Angie avoided shops where they sold teen fashion. In the previous few years, she had bought Tia clothes for Christmas and the shops would be a painful reminder of the family's loss. 'She was a real girly girl,' she said. 'And I know that this Christmas would have been all about clothes, hair and nails for Tia. So it is very upsetting when I have to walk past those things knowing I could have been buying them for her. You just have to think about the good times which we were lucky enough to have.'

Although Tia had reached an age where she no longer

believed in Father Christmas, she had maintained the illusion for her younger brothers and made a point of counting down the days to Christmas itself: 'She helped to make Christmas magical for Jack and Harry. I really feel for those boys, not having her around this year. It's going to be so difficult. I remember last year she was so excited at seeing the boys open their presents. But I know Tia will be looking down on us from heaven this year, making sure we all have a peaceful Christmas.'

While Angie at times claimed she planned to spend Christmas Day alone, she also said she expected to meet up with her son David, Natalie Sharp and their two sons on the 25th in the memorial garden built for Tia, to lay flowers in her memory.

'Obviously they've got the boys to think about, so they will want to make their day special,' said Mrs Niles. 'But I quite like the idea of being alone at home. I know it sounds morbid but maybe having a quiet day to remember Tia will do me some good. I know David and Natalie have a big picture of her in their home. So when her brothers are opening their presents, Tia will be watching just like she once would have.

'That's why we decided to write the letter. It's the first year when we won't have Tia's wonderful personality to make us laugh but we want her to know she is always with us. It just felt like the right thing to do. As much as it breaks our hearts that she isn't here, we'll never forget her.'

More loose ends were being tied up. Finally, on 6 February 2013, neighbour Paul Meehan was charged with wasting police time. Any indication that he was in some way involved in either the murder or the cover-up had now been categorically denied. In court on 28 February, he also denied making false reports while the police searched for Tia, and at the time of writing he was awaiting trial for this charge. The following week, Hazell appeared in Court One of the Old Bailey, again via video link from Belmarsh. He pleaded not guilty to murder and was remanded in custody to face trial in the same court in May. Natalie Sharp, David Niles and Stephen Carter watched from the public gallery. Still Hazell had not faced his accusers but he would not be able to escape that fate for ever. In May he would have to appear in an open courtroom where Tia's family would be present. There would be no hiding place then.

But a month before Hazell finally appeared in court, another story surfaced that had disturbing parallels, which would become apparent at Hazell's trial. It concerned Tia and April Jones, a five-year-old who had gone missing in Powys on 1 October 2012. Newspaper articles about the two girls were found in the bedroom of would-be pop singer and paedophile Opemipo Jaji, who had been convicted of the rape of an 11-year-old schoolgirl in a London park. He also kept a copy of a book about the repeated rape of underage girls. The court at his trial for rape was told that 18-year-old Jaji, a trainee chef, was 'obsessed with little white girls' and that he used Facebook to trawl images from all over the world. On his own page, he wrote, 'Warning. Dangerously sexy person owns this page.'

He reeled in victims from all over the world by linking the Facebook page to fan websites for the Disney children's television series *Hannah Montana* and the film *My Sister's Keeper*, which was about an 11-year-old girl.

In November 2012 Jaji had seen his victim on the bus on her way home from school. When she got off in Enfield, he alighted too and followed her. She crossed the road three times then started to run to get away. Chasing after the child, he grabbed her and dragged her to a secluded part of Jubilee Park where he forced her to strip off her school uniform, then shoved a glove in her mouth and raped her repeatedly. Her ordeal lasted three hours. The girl tried to escape twice but Jaji threatened to kill her.

The attack took place just 90 minutes after he had seen his probation officer. Unlike Hazell, Jaji had previous convictions for sexual offences. Indeed, he had been convicted of another sex attack on a young girl in the same area of north London a year earlier. In court, he admitted to sexually assaulting a 12-year-old white girl there in September 2011. Again he had followed the victim from the bus stop, then taken her to housing estate where he had forced her to strip, stuffed a tie in her mouth and started to abuse her, but that time he had stopped when disturbed by a passer-by.

For that offence, he was given a 10-month detention and training order. As he was under 18 and had been sentenced to less than 12 months' custody, his name did not have to appear on the sex offenders' register. Released after 5 months in April 2012, he was fined £15 for failing to comply with the training order.

The following month more than 600 indecent images of underage white girls were found on his MP4 player. He had been downloading the most obscene category of child-abuse images. This time he was given an 18-month youth-rehabilitation order requiring him to be supervised by the probation service and he was ordered to carry out 50 hours' unpaid work. Then in September he pleaded guilty to an offence of making an indecent image of a child, and was given another community sentence.

But when he appeared in the Old Bailey in April 2013 for the rape of the 11-year-old in London, he did not plead guilty, despite overwhelming DNA evidence. This forced his victim to give testimony and relive the horrific attack. 'I'm not capable of doing something as despicable and heartless as this,' he told the court.

Rosina Cottage QC, for the prosecution, accused him of wanting to proceed with the trial so he could get sexual gratification from hearing the girl recount her ordeal.

The court was shown CCTV footage of him watching the girl from the back of a bus as she chatted excitedly with a school friend. Jaji never denied that he was on the bus and followed her.

The girl told the court, 'I saw the man and he was in front of me. Then I crossed the road. I walked fast so I could get ahead of him and crossed the road again. He was behind me and I crossed the road again for a third time. He started following again so I ran.'

But she could not outrun the 18-year-old, who overpowered her.

She went on to recount the bewildering conversation that took place during the assault. 'He said he didn't want to do this,' she recalled, 'but he was being made to do it to protect his family. I said, "Why?" He didn't say anything.

He just said, "Shut up!" again. He said, "I'm this close to killing you." He said he was going to let me go but I couldn't tell anyone or he would stab me.'

He also threatened to film the rape and send copies to children at her school and 'everyone she loved'. Images of her naked would be circulated if she did not do what he wanted. At one point help seemed to be at hand when a dog walker passed by. But Jaji ordered the terrified girl to crouch down and said, 'Stop moving or I'll stab you.'

Her parents, who expected her home at 5pm, were soon frantic with worry. It was only at around 8pm that Jaji told the girl, 'If I were you, I'd run.' She did and arrived home 'dishevelled, dirty and panicky', the court was told.

During the trial, the girl's father revealed how his traumatised daughter came home and said, 'I think I've been raped.' He continued, 'As you can imagine, we were devastated by what she had said. I had my arm around her. She was shivering.'

During a medical examination, including one under general anaesthetic, the victim was found to have suffered 'bruising, swelling and tearing'. She required emergency surgery for severe injuries she had suffered during the attack and was in hospital for two days.

The police found traces of the girl's blood about 150 yards (137 metres) from the park entrance. Two days later, a local Police Community Support Officer realised that the description given by the victim matched Jaji and he was arrested. Officers noted that he kept cracking his knuckles, something the 11-year-old had told police her attacker had done during the assault. Forensic evidence soon backed up the officer's hunch when traces of the victim's blood were found on his bag and trainers. The analysis of mobile-phone records placed Jaji at the park – during the attack, he had sent a text message. CCTV footage showed him on a bus returning from college and later at a youth club but he didn't feature on any security footage during the time of the assault.

When police raided the home that Jaji shared with his mother in Edmonton, they discovered adverts from parents looking for childminders, and for apprenticeships in childcare, in his bedroom, along with the articles about Tia and April, and the pornography material. On his bed they found a paperback called *Nobody Cared* about a young girl who was sexually abused, and a picture of a seven-year-old hung on his bedroom wall.

In her summing up, Rosina Cottage described Jaji as a 'deliberate and manipulative sexual predator… [who] brutally terrified and raped her and then casually went to youth club… while she was being taken to hospital.'

Jaji was born in north London, although he claimed to be from Lagos, Nigeria. He was training to be a chef at the De Vere Academy of Hospitality in Greenwich, south-east London, but boasted that he was such a talented singer that he had been invited to appear on BBC One's *The Voice* talent show.

Following the conviction, Sarah Maclaren of the Crown Prosecution Service saluted the little girl who had the courage to testify against him court: 'I would like to thank the 11-year-old victim and her family for their enormous strength and courage in supporting this prosecution,' she said.

She also described the rape as a 'vicious and horrific

attack' and said, 'A dangerous sexual offender has now been brought to justice.' Another count of rape and one of attempted rape were to be left lying on his file, which could be reactivated if he offended again.

After the trial, Detective Chief Inspector Adam Lowe described Jaji as a 'time-bomb ready to go off', adding, 'Jaji posed a great danger to young girls and, despite the great weight of evidence against him, refused to accept his guilt and forced the victim to give evidence in court. This was a particularly brutal but unusual attack on an innocent 11-year-old schoolgirl who will, no doubt, continue to suffer the emotional scars of what happened to her for a very long time.'

Though Jaji would go to jail for a very long time, it was clear that mistakes had been made. MP for Edmonton Andy Love told the *Daily Mail*, 'I'm shocked by the admissions that have come out since the guilty verdict. It's amazing that this girl had to go through such a brutal and horrific attack when it was clear that this young man had quite a long history of deviant sexual behaviour. Clearly, we need a proper investigation into what happened. We need to know what sort of supervision he was under. This young man was going seriously wrong. Why wasn't that picked up?'

Having committed a similar offence before and exhibiting a palpable sexual interest in young girls, it is shocking that he was allowed to walk the streets. A spokesman for the Ministry of Justice said there would be two reviews of the handling of Jaji by the authorities. The first would be a Multi Agency Public Protection Arrangements – or MAPPA – case review that would examine his all-round supervision, including the time he was under the supervision of the Youth Offending Team following his sexual-assault conviction in 2011. Then a 'Serious Further Offence' review would look at the 11-week period he was under supervision after his conviction for possession of indecent images.

The Ministry of Justice reviews would also look into whether Jaji should have been officially registered as a sex offender after the sexual assault conviction. If he had been, police would have been able to conduct home visits and they may have discovered the articles and pictures in his bedroom showing that he had a sexual interest in prepubescent girls.

CHAPTER TEN

DISTURBING
PARALLELS

It took nine months for Stuart Hazell to come to trial. During that time there were two other cases that demonstrated disturbing parallels.

In February 2013, Mick Philpott and his wife Mairead went to trial for the manslaughter of their six children, who had burned to death in a fire at their home in the Derby suburb of Allenton. Like Hazell, Philpott had courted publicity over the case and invented an entirely fictional version of events, which he fed to the media. The couple had appeared at an emotional press conference after the fire, weeping copiously as they described the blaze, though it was later discovered that they had started it themselves.

Also like Hazell, Philpott had a long criminal record behind him, including convictions for crimes of violence. At the age of 21, he was absent without leave from the army when he had tried to kill his then-girlfriend. She had sent Philpott a letter breaking off the two-year relationship. He crept into her family home and attacked her with a knife as she lay in bed, stabbing her 27 times with the 9-inch blade. He also stabbed her mother when she intervened. His girlfriend suffered collapsed lungs, and punctured bladder, kidney and liver. She blames the attack for the liver cancer she suffered later. Doctors believe that the rare cancer that is killing her was triggered by the scar tissue from the lacerated organ.

When ambulance men rode to the rescue, they found Philpott lounging on the stairs, still holding the flick knife that was dripping with blood.

'You're wasting your time with that one,' he said. 'I've done a good job on her. She's a goner.'

Philpott was given seven years for the attempted murder, with a concurrent five years for causing grievous bodily harm with intent to the mother. The judge said he was 'a dangerous young man'.

From prison, he wrote to her saying, 'No hard feelings. When I get out, you and I can get married like we always planned to.' She burned the letter.

Philpott was released after just three years and two months, and she said she lived in 'fear and dread' of ever seeing him again.

He then married Pamela Lomax, who gave him two children. She told police she would 'do anything for a peaceful life' and prayed that he would find someone else. Thirty-seven-year-old Philpott then met 14-year-old Heather Kehoe. According to Heather's testimony at Philpott's trial, the pair were caught by Pamela Lomax having sex in the couple's marital bed. Philpott then issued an ultimatum to Kehoe – she should either go back to her disapproving parents or flee with him to Derby. So on her 16th birthday she ran away from her parents to move in with him.

She soon fell pregnant but this did not stop Philpott pinning her to the floor and abusing her whenever he pleased. In a short space of time, Kehoe gave birth to two children, both boys; 'He wanted a girl,' Heather told the court at his trial. 'He used to beat me for that.' When she tried to leave him, he held a knife to her throat, telling her that he would do to her what he had done to his previous girlfriend.

'Mick was leaving me in no doubt he would do the same to me,' she said.

He also encouraged their elder son to verbally abuse and punch her. And as 'punishment', he would throw her out in the garden at night and she said she 'would curl up in the outside toilet until he would let [her] back in again.'

In 1991 he received a two-year conditional discharge for assault causing actual bodily harm after he head-butted a colleague. Then in 2000 he met 19-year-old Mairead Duffy, a single mother. She soon moved into Philpott's council house in Victory Road and they married in 2003.

However, Philpott had already met 16-year-old single mother Lisa Willis. He was then in his forties. Philpott invited Willis to move into the house he was sharing with Duffy and a relationship between them began, along with episodes of violence. He hit her repeatedly with a piece of wood, insisting that the father of her son was someone other than who she said it was. Nevertheless, Willis was a bridesmaid at Philpott and Duffy's wedding.

Meanwhile, Kehoe was fighting Philpott for custody of their two children and on 23 December 2002 she won.

In 2006 Philpott came to the attention of the press when he asked for a bigger council house to accommodate his wife, his mistress and their 14 children. Both women were pregnant at the time. The three-bedroom house was cramped, he said. His wife worked as a part-time domestic assistant. Otherwise they lived on £510 a week in benefits. He defended this lifestyle on *The Jeremy Kyle Show*, where he said he intended to divorce his wife and marry his mistress Lisa Willis so that she could share the Philpott name. He purported to be a good dad who looked after his kids because press exposure of his criminal record prevented him getting a job.

Philpott said he could not understand why people were shocked at the way his family lived, even though he revealed intimate details of the sexual dynamics involved. He would spend alternate nights with his wife and his mistress in the caravan in his garden.

'You lot are criticising us for being as a threesome,' Philpott lashed out. 'We don't do threesomes, full-stop.' So why did people feel disgust?

Philpott was now seen by the tabloids as Britain's greatest scrounger. So next he appeared in a documentary, *Ann Widdecombe Versus the Benefits Culture*, where the former Conservative minister spent a week with him and tried to get him to change his lifestyle and get a job. Although the local paper gleefully ran the headline TORY ANN MOVES IN WITH DAD OF 17 ON BENEFITS, Ms Widdecombe refused to join him in the caravan. She did manage to find him three potential jobs, resulting in an offer of employment with Burton-based barrel maker Cammac Brewery Support Services. The company later withdrew its offer when Philpott failed to turn up.

By then his television antics had earned him the tabloid nickname 'Shameless Mick'.

In 2010 he was given a police caution after slapping Mairead and dragging her outside by her hair. Soon after, Philpott pleaded guilty to common assault following a road rage incident where he punched another driver, after nearly killing seven of his children who were in the car during his manic pursuit.

In February 2011 Lisa Willis left the communal home to live with her sister and brother-in-law, taking with her the four children by Philpott and her older son, who had a different father.

On the night of 11 May 2012 Mairead had sex with family friend Paul Mosley on the family's snooker table after a friendly game. Philpott then joined in. They had all been smoking cannabis. The house later caught fire with the children trapped upstairs. At the time it was said that Philpott made 'valiant attempts' to save them but it was later reported that he had only smacked ineffectively at the double-glazed window with a child's tennis racquet while neighbours exhibited true heroism and risked their lives. Mairead was completely physically unaffected by the fire, while Philpott showed nothing more than a little reddening of the skin. It was also noticed that they were remarkably clean for a couple who had been fighting to rescue their children from a fire.

The death toll was tragic. Five of their children died in

the flames, another died later in hospital. All perished from smoke inhalation, post-mortems established.

Fire investigators then found petrol under the letterbox, indicating that the fire had been started deliberately, and a murder investigation was opened. Forensic analysis revealed that the petrol was of a type sold at Total garages. It had been poured not through the letterbox of the PVC front door but used to dowse the floor from within the hallway.

Assistant Chief Constable Steve Cotterill said, 'Initial indications are that it was deliberately set and, as a result, six children have been unlawfully killed. The forensic examination is still continuing. A number of specialists, including fingerprints officers, have been examining the scene and this is likely to continue for some time. We have yet to speak in detail with Mr and Mrs Philpott and that will happen sometime this week as, understandably, the couple are distraught at the loss of their six children.'

A group of local businessmen offered a reward to help catch those responsible for setting the fire, while Mikey Philpott, half-brother to the six children killed, called for 'justice' in the press. 'It's tearing us to pieces that they have gone just like that,' he said. 'It's been really hard to take it all in. I've broken down a few times. I'd like justice for my brothers and sisters more than anything – it is strung out that someone can just do something like that.'

He described how he had discovered that his siblings were dead.

'I knew there was something wrong as soon as I saw there had been a fire,' he said. 'I rang my dad and it went straight to voicemail. Then I rang Mairead and there was nothing. Then I rang my step-brother, Richard, and went straight off to hospital. Everyone was around us. When I went around to see my grandma, I've never been squeezed so tight. But the support we have had so far, from everyone, is amazing.'

Mikey had not lived with the family after his mother won custody in 2002. Nevertheless, he said, 'I was pretty close to my brothers and sisters. I didn't realise how close until I lost them. Duwayne was a great brother. I spent a lot of time fishing with him at weekends. Jade was a proper daddy's girl, always smiling. You could never get John to shut up, bless him. He was really playful. Then there was Jessie. You couldn't get five minutes alone without her; she was always clinging on to your leg. It was the same with Jaden. Jack was like me, a proper computer nerd, always on his Nintendo DS.'

He said he really missed them. 'They were like my best friends, always there for me and keeping a smile on my face. But now they are not here.'

Philpott told the press that the family had been 'overwhelmed' with support from the local community. A service was held in the local Roman Catholic Church and the charity Catch Me When I Fall was set up by local residents to support the family.

'We grew up in a community that's been through a lot of problems with violence and to see this community come together like it has, it's too overwhelming,' said Philpott. 'Those poor gentlemen from the fire brigade, who saw what we saw – my heart goes out to them.'

As with Stuart Hazell, Philpott's statements to the media were all lies. And he also made an appeal for privacy. 'Please leave my family alone,' he said. 'If you've got any questions or anything at all, please don't come through me and my family, please go to the police. You're disrupting what these officers are trying to do. So please, I beg you, leave us alone and let us try and grieve in peace and quiet.'

However, ACC Cotterill was surprised at how unhelpful the community were being. 'While I thank those members of the community who have come forward with information,' he said, 'I am surprised by how few people have contacted us. Normally, in cases of this scale, more information is passed to the police. I strongly suspect that there is someone out there in the community who knows more than we are being told.'

Nonetheless, the community held a vigil for the dead children, releasing Chinese lanterns into the night sky. But one family member secretly voiced their suspicions. They told the *Daily Mail*, 'Lisa and Mick broke up a few months ago and she went to stay with Ian and Amanda for a few days before moving to a hostel and then on to another home on the other side of Derby.'

The fire had broken out the very day a custody hearing for Lisa Willis's children was to have been held. Suspicion soon turned on Philpott. It was noted that the couple never entered the specialist burns unit where their son Duwayne lay dying. Relatives reported that they engaged in food fights at the hospital and went on a shopping spree while the community was raising funds for the funerals. They were also said to have sung 'Suspicious Minds' in a pub karaoke session.

Mairead Philpott's sister Jennifer Lobban said the couple

were 'discussing where to order Chinese and complaining that the hospital was crap because it had not provided them with food, just a room to sleep… I was getting phone calls every day saying they were out, they were shopping and, from that moment on, I did not want to see them anymore. The lack of respect for the kids, it was disgusting.'

Marie Smith, mortuary manager at Derby Royal Hospital, spoke out about how Philpott appeared to pretend to faint when he saw the children's bodies for the first time and later engaged in horseplay with a police family-liaison officer who he put into a headlock.

Smith told Sky News that Philpott also once referred to the young victims as 'little shits' and requested gin when she offered him water. The parents' visits were like a 'circus', said Smith. 'To me, it didn't quite match that he was coming to see his children who had died and he was engaging in horseplay – it was almost like it was a social event.'

Witnesses from the scene of the blaze then began to voice awkward questions. Why had Philpott been convinced that all the children would be in one room around the back of the house? It seems that it was from there that Philpott and Mosley were intending to rescue them. In fact, their bodies were found in all three bedrooms. They had quickly been overcome by the 'chimney effect' caused by the fire in the hallway sucking in air through the lounge window, sending smoke rushing up the stairs and out of the bedroom windows.

Detective Superintendent Kate Meynell interviewed the Philpotts' neighbours who had also tried to rescue the children that night. 'Within a few days they commented on how they felt they were making more effort to rescue the children and that Michael Philpott was not as instrumental as he should have been,' she said.

All agreed that he seemed to be enjoying the attention. It was an observation also made by ACC Cotterill, an officer with 30 years' experience. He said that, while it was hard to define what constitutes normal behaviour in the midst of a tragedy of such magnitude, it was apparent that Philpott was acting unusually. 'I have more or less given up trying to explain his behaviour,' said ACC Cotterill. 'It doesn't fit within the limits of normality. I believe any parent would have made the ultimate sacrifice in those circumstances. He didn't.'

Later he said, 'I would have expected him to be completely and utterly destroyed.' Instead, Cotterill said, it was like watching an actor playing a part. 'It was a sham, in my view.'

This aroused such suspicion that, at its height, 88 police officers were working on the case. They seized more than 2,410 exhibits and took over 5,000 statements. In the absence of any concrete evidence, the police decided to bug the room in the Premier Inn where the Philpotts were staying. The tapes caught Mairead and Mosley having sex to cement their diabolical pact.

It seems that Philpott had enjoyed his appearance on *The Jeremy Kyle Show* so much that he wanted to run his own media campaign and was unusually insistent in his desire to hold a press conference.

On 16 May, some 80 journalists were assembled at a hotel in Derby. Police had doubts about letting the event to go ahead at all. As it turned out, it lasted just a couple of minutes before the couple appeared to be overwhelmed by all the hoopla. After what senior officers saw as a 'shameful' appearance in front of the media, Philpott again pretended to collapse backstage. However, the police were listening in on the couple's conversations there too and heard them agree to continue in their collusion.

'You make sure you stick to your story,' Philpott was recorded saying. 'They're not gonna find any evidence, are they? You know what I mean?'

Forensic evidence began to stack up against the couple too. A petrol can had been found nearby Victory Road along with a glove. Then petrol was found on Philpott's clothes and on leggings and a thong owned by Mairead. More petrol was found in the U-bend of the kitchen sink.

The Philpotts were arrested and charged with murder on 28 May 2012. Later another witness, Melissa John, the partner of Mosley's nephew, came forward to describe how Mosley had confessed to having staged a rehearsal of the fire six weeks before the blaze. On 5 November Mosley, too, was charged with the children's murder after a fresh forensic examination of the petrol on his clothing. He said it had been spilled when he was filling up his car at a BP garage, but it was Total petrol that was found on his clothing. He had no explanation for this.

In the end, the Crown Prosecution Service downgraded the charges against all three to manslaughter. Although the accused had been incomprehensibly stupid, investigators concluded they had not meant to kill their children. Instead, they had intended to stage a dramatic rescue. The aim was to hit back at Willis for leaving him, while turning themselves into both victims and heroes. Those close to the case said the three had showed no genuine remorse at any stage during the investigation and believed throughout that they would get away with it.

The trial began at Nottingham Crown Court on 12 February 2013 while Hazell was still being held on remand. They pleaded not guilty to six counts of manslaughter. The incriminating tapes were played in court and the jury found all three defendants guilty. The judge, Mrs Justice Thirlwall, said Philpott hatched a plot to frame Willis for an arson attack on the family home on the eve of a child-custody hearing.

'It was a wicked and dangerous plan,' she said. 'And you put it into effect with the assistance of your two co-defendants. You poured petrol on the floor. Paul Mosley was responsible for removing the containers from your home. You set light to it. After a short while, Mairead Philpott spoke to the emergency services. It became clear there was no chance of a successful rescue and the children perished. Mercifully, their deaths were swift and, it would seem, without pain.'

Mick Philpott was sentenced to life with a minimum tariff of 15 years. Whether he would ever be released, the judge said, was a matter for the parole board. Paul Mosley and Mairead Philpott were each sentenced to 17 years; they must serve at least half of it before being released on licence. Mairead later appealed her sentence.

In the north, the Philpotts had inspired almost as much hatred as Hazell had in London. As the trio were sentenced, there were shouts from the public gallery of 'Die, Mick, die'. Philpott made an obscene hand gesture as he was led away to prison.

'This is the saddest case I have ever dealt with. It is the most tragic case. I have felt very angry at the loss of life,' observed ACC Cotterill. 'There are six little children that have not got the chance to grow up.'

They would be missed, particularly at school. 'Six empty chairs must have been horrendous for the teachers and the children. How do you tell them they won't be here tomorrow or next Monday because their mum and dad have chosen to light a fire at the bottom of the stairs and killed them?' he said.

Tia Sharp would similarly be missed at school.

Another child who will not grow up is five-year-old April Jones. She went missing just two months after Tia and was playing on her bike with her best friend near their homes on Bryn-y-Gog estate near the town of Machynlleth in Powys when she vanished. Although she suffered from cerebral palsy, she was in year one at school and was doing well. Her condition did not stop her having a full and active life.

Her disappearance, like Tia's, sparked a massive hunt. April's body was never found, despite the biggest search operation in British policing history. Then Mark Bridger, a man known to the family, was arrested for her murder. He was a man strikingly similar to Hazell – a drinker, a drug user and a fantasist who scoured the Internet for kiddie porn, as we will see at Hazell's trial.

The police found April's blood in his home and, on the computer, were pictures of April and her teenage half-sisters. It was said that he had gone online looking for pictures of underage girls being forced to have sex, and launched Internet searches for 'naked young five-year-old and ten-year-old girls', 'nudism five-year-old' and 'France: British schoolgirl raped and murdered'. These included images that depicted 'adults having sex with girls, some consensual, some non-consensual'.

The former slaughterhouse man, who also previously worked as a lifeguard and welder, also kept files on his computer of high-profile murders. They included images of Soham victims Holly Wells and Jessica Chapman, Caroline Dickinson – the British schoolgirl murdered in a French hostel in 1996 – and Jessica Lunsford – a nine-year-old American girl who was abducted in Florida in 2005.

April Jones disappeared on 1 October 2012, less than ten weeks after Tia Sharp had gone missing. Mark Bridger went on trial on 29 April 2013 at Mold Crown Court, just a week before Stuart Hazell entered the dock of the Old Bailey. April's parents turned up at court hand in hand. They wore pink ribbons. Her father, Paul Jones, wore a pink shirt and her mother had her hair died pink. It was said to be April's favourite colour and they had vowed to wear pink every day in the hope that their daughter might be found.

Bridger, who had a coiled cobra tattooed on his forearm, was charged with abduction, murder and perverting the course of justice by disposing of, concealing or destroying April's body – all of which he denied. However, he admitted being responsible for her death. He said he had run her over by accident with his Land Rover while she was out on her bike. He was drunk and panicked but then said he had no recollection of what he had done with the body.

The prosecution began its case by playing the court a harrowing 999 call made by April's mother Coral Jones. Mrs Jones could be heard saying, 'Please... please, my daughter has been kidnapped... my daughter.'

The call was then taken over by a neighbour, who said, 'Apparently, what happened... she has gone off in a car with somebody. Somebody has picked her up in a car or something. I have not seen anything, I have just been told.'

The operator then asked to speak to Coral again. There were a series of long pauses where people can be heard crying and hyperventilating in a state of obvious distress. This was so affecting that some members of the jury were physically upset. In the dock, Bridger shook his head, trying to hold back tears. Then he took a deep breath and wiped them from his eyes.

PC Fiona Evans arrived at April's home at 7.37pm to speak to a witness who saw April getting into a vehicle, which the prosecution say was Bridger's Land Rover. The witness thought that the little girl knew the man that took her. She said she saw April get in the driver's door and climb into the back of the vehicle. 'I couldn't hear anything,' the witness told the officer. 'I didn't say anything. I just watched. I thought she'd come back.'

Later she said, 'April had a happy face as she got into the vehicle.'

Despite Bridger's denials, blood and bone were found in the lounge, hallway and bathroom of his home three miles outside the market town of Machynlleth in Wales where April lived. The DNA matches that of April. Bridger claimed he had no recollection of taking her there either dead or dying. The prosecution said that he was already trying to clean April's blood from the rooms as hundreds of volunteers were scouring streets and countryside in the hope of finding her alive.

Forensic scientist Emma Howes not only found numerous drops of blood that matched April's DNA but also a 'drip trail' of bloodstains under the living room carpet and leading to the hallway. 'The blood from April Jones was present in various areas of the carpet,' she said. 'These stains were not readily visible on the top surface. The larger stain, near the fireplace, appeared to have soaked through from the top of the carpet to the underneath... This soaking and staining indicates that the carpet has been in prolonged contact with a source of April Jones' wet blood.'

She said that this came from April herself, rather than some other object wet with her blood. 'This staining is what I would expect if April herself had been lying in this area for some period of time shedding blood.'

While there was a 'considerable amount of blood' on the carpet, Ms Howes said it was her opinion that 'attempts' had been made to 'remove the blood present in this area'. She added, 'Someone or something wet with the blood of April Jones has moved across the carpet, dripping blood as they moved.'

The court heard that a trail appeared to lead from the lounge to the hallway and then into the bathroom where more traces of April's blood were found on the shower curtain, on the hot tap and on a washing machine. Ms Howes said these traces of blood 'would indicate' that a person has 'attempted to clean blood from themselves or from a blood-stained object'.

Two pieces of carpet and a bath mat were found in the river that runs behind Bridger's cottage but no bodily fluids were found on them. 'However,' Ms Howes added, 'it should be noted that these items were recovered from the river and were in a poor condition and it may be possible that evidence may have been lost.'

Another forensic scientist, Andrew Parry, said the blood found in the living room was entirely consistent with April being on the floor and blood seeping from an injury, through the carpet and on to the floor below.

'All I can tell you is blood drained from at least one injury,' he said.

The bloodstains also indicated that 'some activity happened in the bathroom'. Either the body or some item stained with wet blood had been taken in there. There were also indications that an attempt had been made to clean up the blood.

When officers first turned up at his hillside home, Mount Pleasant Cottage, in Ceinws, they were greeted with the strong smell of cleaning products. Inside there were cans of strong cider.

Initially, the police searched the house to see if April was hiding there. As in the case of Tia Sharp, they were hunting for a missing person at that time. April's disappearance only became a murder case later.

The police also noticed a wood-burning stove in the living room. It was 3pm in the middle of the summer but Detective Constable Sarah Totterdale immediately saw that there was a fire in the log burner. She said the heat was 'noticeable' as soon as she walked in and the stove was 'glowing an orange colour'. She said, 'It hadn't just been lit. This fire had obviously been burning for some time. It was uncomfortably hot because I was perspiring in the room and I only had a thin raincoat on.'

Fragments of a juvenile skull were recovered from the ashes and, nearby, specks of April's blood were found, the court was told. There were 18 bone fragments in all – 17 were burned and in the log burner and the 18th, which was not burned, was recovered from the plughole in the bathroom.

The former abattoir worker's boning knife was found near the stove. It had a charred handle and burn marks on the blade. The jury were later shown around the cottage, where flowers and a teddy had been left in April's memory.

Gage Talbot, a colleague at Randall Parker Foods where Bridger worked as a slaughterman, said, 'Mark Bridger's employment would have allowed him access to an array of knives, and he was skilled with boning and skinning knives.'

Prosecuting counsel Miss Elwen Evans QC told the jury that Bridger was 'forensically aware' and went to extensive lengths to remove potentially incriminating evidence while disposing of the body. On their tour of the cottage, the jury were shown the spots of blood picked out by forensic experts with green arrows.

Some 13 hours after April disappeared, Bridger was seen near a roadside layby carrying a black bin bag.

Emma Howes also examined Bridger's Land Rover Discovery. She said there was 'no evidence to indicate that April had been hit' by the car as Bridger claimed. He had said that he put the child in his car after running her over. But Ms Howes said she found 'no signs to indicate that

April Jones had been bleeding freely whilst inside' the vehicle. But traces of semen found in the Land Rover showed that 'some form of sexual activity' may have happened in the car, although there was no evidence to indicate that this involved April. However, April's DNA was found in the 'crotch area' of Bridger's jogging bottoms.

Forensic scientists used April's toothbrush to obtain her DNA.

'One didn't have April to take a DNA profile in the usual way,' they said.

The police also seized an axe and two swords from Bridger's cottage but no traces of blood or DNA were found on them.

On her first visit, DC Totterdale had noticed a strong smell of washed clothes and washing powder downstairs, and a chemical smell in the air. She identified this as the smell of cleaning products and detergent, which appeared strongest in the living room and towards the bathroom.

When Bridger was arrested on 2 October, the day after April's disappearance, he had said, 'I know what it's all about.'

PC Phil Saunders then said he asked him, 'Where is she?'

Unlike Hazell, Bridger did not deny that he was responsible: 'It was an accident. I crushed her with the car. I don't know where she is.'

During their journey to Aberystwyth police station, Bridger told the officer, 'I have been looking for her all night and today on foot because my vehicle is in the garage. It is a left-hand drive Land Rover Discovery. I didn't abduct her. I did my best to revive her. I panicked... I didn't even know until this morning who she was until

I saw the television... I just wish I knew what I had done to her, where I put her. I want to say sorry to the family.'

Bridger said that he could not believe that he had not called an ambulance or police, said PC Saunders. According to the police officer, Bridger then said, 'There was no life in her, no response, no breath, no response in her eyes. She was just on the seat. I tried to revive her,' he said.

But he was insistent that he could not remember what he had done with her and said he had looked through all the rooms in the house. 'I would not have dumped her,' Bridger told the officer. 'She is a human being. I would not have done that.'

He told the police that he 'could have burned the body' but he could not remember. Bridger, who had also once been a fireman in London, said he would have 'laid her to rest... out of respect' so that the body could be found and that he may have covered her with a tarpaulin sheet.

Detention officer Stephen Carr said, 'Then he went on to say that he could have burned the body but, with his fire-fighter training, he informed me that burning flesh smells like pork. He said the flesh would smell and his clothing would smell and that he would remember having set a fire.'

Bridger told an interviewing police officer that he could not remember how he had disposed of April's body but that he did not think he would have taken her out of the car, as someone would have seen him.

Bridger told police, 'They would have lynched me. They would have got hold of me.' Faced with a hostile crowd, he would have had to 'prove then what I want to prove to you. That I crushed her and I gave her as much medical attention as I could.'

Bridger denied that the attack was sexually motivated.

'I'm 95 per cent impotent,' he said, and his ex-girlfriend Vicky Fenner had dumped him hours before April disappeared as he could not perform sexually. He told the court this had a lot to do with his consumption of alcohol. He told police, 'I'm a registered alcoholic who drinks 15 to 20 pints a day and half a bottle to a bottle of vodka a day.'

In court he said actually drank 16 to 25 cans of cider a day and a bottle to a bottle and a half of wine. But on certain occasions, when he was 'really down or bad', he would buy vodka. This included the day before April went missing.

Asked if he had ever registered as an alcoholic, he said he had 'picked the phone up a number of times and spoken to people... I don't think I ever registered... I spoke to my doctor and said that I had a problem.'

He also said that he had been taking anti-depressants on and off for 12 years and that the child porn on his computer was there because he was trying 'to understand the changes my daughter is going through'. He said that he gained no sexual gratification from them. An indecent cartoon was also found on his computer. Bridger said he had kept them to complain to the companies responsible for publishing them after coming across them accidentally while looking up 'cartoon things' for his daughter. 'She was into SpongeBob SquarePants. I came across this. That's why I was concerned,' he said.

One of the online cartoons that he viewed on the day

April went missing showed the rape of a girl who was physically restrained and visibly in distress.

Asked how he felt looking at pictures of the five-year-old April on his PC, he allegedly told police, 'Fucked up. It bloody frightens me. I know what I've done and, if I remember where she is, I will tell you.'

The day April went missing, Bridger had viewed a large number of pictures of a 14-year-old girl from the Machynlleth area on Facebook. He explained that one of his sons was in a relationship with a local girl and had got her pregnant. Bridger said he was looking at pictures of local girls to see if he could work out which one she was.

One of the pictures he viewed that day was of April. Bridger said he did not know who she was 'until this case came up and I was shown the pictures'. However, April's mother Coral had once been Bridger's friend on Facebook but his former partner Vicky Fenner had made him delete Mrs Jones while they were together. The jury were then told that Coral Jones requested to be friends on the social networking site a second time, some time after she had been removed from his contacts.

The court also heard evidence from a 10-year-old girl who said she had been out playing with her friend. 'I saw Mark in his car and he offered me to have a sleepover with his daughter at his house,' she said. 'He parked up and spoke to me.'

She said Mr Bridger 'got his window down' and started talking to her.

'He asked me if I could go and have a sleepover with his daughter.'

She knew Bridger. 'I have seen him a couple of times,' she said. 'He's been very nice to me and said hi, how am I doing.'

However, she realised it was a 'bit odd' that he offered her a sleepover but said she answered, 'That'll be great.' No firm arrangements were made. Bridger then left after the conversation, she said. But later she saw Bridger 'five or ten minutes later' near an area where she knew April played on her bike.

She said she saw him in his car 'lying down with a newspaper on his lap with a walkie-talkie in his hand'. She said he got up when he saw her and she smiled at him. Earlier, she had seen April and her friend nearby.

'They were just playing on their bikes,' she said.

She said she then cycled home, had her dinner and went back to see if he was still there but he had gone.

A 'happy and smiling' April was later seen getting into Bridger's Land Rover. As the vehicle sat high above the ground, she would have had to have been lifted. While the five-year-old was of 'slight build', he was of 'big build… over six feet tall and very strong'.

Bridger was a fantasist. He told doctors that his parents were dead when, in fact, they were still alive. He also claimed that he was an SAS-trained mercenary, who'd seen action in Angola. After being trained by an SAS unit in Burma, he said he was seconded to the British Army. The Ministry of Defence had no record of him working for UK Armed Forces. In court he admitted his claims were not true and he had no military experience. He explained, 'When I moved close to the Machynlleth area, everyone seemed to want to know who I was, where I was from, my past, my present. I had always been interested in the military. I just said I was ex-army. I didn't want them to know that I'd had problems in my past. That's stuck with me until now.'

He knew April's parents, Paul and Coral Jones.

'They are friends of mine and I have killed their daughter,' he told the interviewing officers. 'I did everything wrong.'

Explaining the bone fragments in his log burner, he said that he had picked up his two youngest children two days before April went missing. They had gone for a mountain walk to pick mushrooms. Returning to his home, he had cooked a chicken on the wood stove.

'We cooked it and ate it and anything left over gets thrown in the fire. This has happened on a number of occasions,' he said. However, he said that he cleaned out the ashes 'every day or every night'.

Referring to his job in the abattoir, he was asked if he was 'constantly cutting meat'. Bridger replied 'no', adding he had 'nothing to do with any knives' at first, saying his job was to 'assess the meat'. He said he then progressed to a side of the business which was more to do with welfare, with testing meat and ensuring the animals were 'respected'.

Like Hazell, Bridger had a long criminal record. When just 19, he pleaded guilty to offences including possession of a firearm, having an imitation firearm with intent to commit an offence, attempting to steal a car, and two counts of obtaining property by deception, using cheques from a stolen cheque book. He appeared at the Old Bailey and was put on probation. He told the jury he had no intention of robbing a post office, as the prosecution at the time claimed.

Bridger got into trouble again in Aberystwyth in 1991 and was convicted of criminal damage, affray and driving without insurance. This had arisen out of a 'road rage' incident where he had struck the bonnet of another car with his hand. The following year, he was convicted of driving while disqualified and without insurance.

He had six children with four different women. After the break-up of the relationship with the mother of his first child, Bridger, who had grown up in south London, quit his job as a fireman and moved to Wales. Homeless, he bought camping and survival equipment and lived on the beach, moving on from time to time.

In 1996 he met Elaine Griffiths, who gave him two children. She had a sister, Karen, who at that time was in a relationship with a man he knew as Paul – the father of April Jones.

'It was through Elaine and Karen I met Paul,' Bridger said.

By 2003 Bridger's relationship with Elaine was breaking down. Police were called on one occasion, which resulted in a conviction for offences that included battery. He was also convicted of threatening a police officer with a machete following a row with an ex-partner.

The relationship came to an end and he moved to Australia but returned to the UK because he missed his children. In April 2007 he pleaded guilty to assault causing actual bodily harm and was sentenced to four months in prison, which was suspended for 18 months. However, he denied having any convictions for sexual offences or downloading indecent images. He also said there had never been any complaints about his behaviour towards his own children or any other youngsters he had contact with.

Each time one of his relationships broke down, he turned to drink and, from early in 2010 until the day he was arrested, Bridger had been drinking heavily. He said he also suffered anxiety and panic attacks. Drinking 'excessively' also resulted in 'lost hours'. 'There were times when I would not know what I did the day before,' he said to the court.

He told how, on the day April vanished, he was drunk by 9.30am. He was upset because his latest relationship had collapsed and he was worried he was going to lose his home. While speaking to the husband of one of his former partners, he said, he'd had to lean against the wall to steady himself.

At around 11.52am, he admitted he'd been browsing for pictures of a local girl he thought might be pregnant with his grandchild. He then looked at the picture of another girl. He did so, he explained, because he thought she might be his daughter. He told jurors how he had once been painting a house with the girl's mother when they 'ended up on the bed together'. Relating the tale, he dabbed his eyes with a tissue.

Other pictures of girls from the Machynlleth area on his laptop that he viewed at 12.07 on 1 October, he said, had been sent to him either by the girl's mother or by her godfather. And another picture of a young child was actually the Facebook profile picture of a friend of his.

Bridger went to a parents' evening that same day. Afterwards he admitted inviting a ten-year-old for a sleepover at his house. He told the jury that, while he had not hosted a sleepover in his Ceinws house, he had hosted them at previous homes.

After the meeting, Bridger went to the Bryn-y-Gog estate that night to see his former girlfriend Vicky Fenner. He said he waited outside her house with the intention of talking to her and didn't knock on her front door because of the relationship he had with her mother. 'I didn't want Vicky to feel like I was haunting her, I just want to talk to her,' he said.

Then Bridger described how he knocked down April. He was just driving off the estate when he felt his car 'rise up on one side'. He continued, 'I didn't travel more than inches and then it rose up. I checked the handbrake was up and I made sure it was in gear, [then] I went to do that a second time and then I realised there was a problem.'

Initially, he'd thought it might have been a piece of wood or breeze-block trapped under his wheel and so got out to have a look. 'I don't know whether I knelt down or bent down to have a look,' he said. 'That's when I saw a little person, a little child that was pushed up against the front wheel.' He then said he 'scooped' the five-year-old from underneath his Land Rover. Her limbs were limp and he tried to perform mouth-to-mouth only to find he 'could not make a seal'.

Bridger was unclear what had happened next. He only remembered driving out of Machynlleth, though he did not remember April being in the car.

'I have no recollection of getting to the house,' he said. 'I have no recollection of taking April into the house. The only other recollection I have is of having April in my arms and laying her down on the carpet.'

What happened next was again a blank.

'I don't remember any clean-up,' Bridger said. 'But what I'd like to say is if, that night, there was blood, drips of blood in the bath where I washed my jumper, if I had seen it, I would automatically have wiped it, not to hide it – it would've been an automatic thing to do.'

He told jurors he remembered taking a beige fleece off before rinsing it in the bath after returning home on the night of 1 October. When he woke the following morning, he said, 'I really thought it was a nightmare or a dream. Then I realised it wasn't a dream, there is something to this. I don't remember exactly what I did. I remember putting some of the clothes I had taken off back on and went outside to search for the little girl.'

Told that the prosecution had suggested he had burned the body in the log burner, he said, 'I don't believe I could do that.'

He had then received a text from his former girlfriend Elaine Dafydd telling him that the police were looking for a left-hand drive vehicle like his Land Rover. Then he simply waited to be arrested. 'I didn't know what to do,' he said. 'I obviously was involved, I didn't ever deny being involved in April's death.' Nevertheless, he said, 'I didn't run, I didn't hide, I didn't go anywhere.'

Bridger said that he expected to be arrested for causing death by reckless or dangerous driving. 'I didn't expect to be on a murder charge,' he said.

Asked, 'Did you abduct April Jones on the Bryn y Gog estate?' he replied, 'No. No. I had no intention of abducting April Jones.'

'Did you have any kind of sexual contact with April Jones that night?'

'No, none at all.'

'Did you deliberately kill April Jones that night?'

'No, I didn't,' he said, wiping the tears from his eyes.

That concluded the case for the prosecution.

CHAPTER ELEVEN

THE CASE AGAINST HAZELL

The trial of Stuart Hazell opened in the Old Bailey on 8 May 2013. Natalie Sharp and Stephen Carter were in the public gallery waiting for proceedings to begin, along with a large contingent of journalists. The judge, Mr Justice Nicol, said that the trial would last between two and three weeks. Mr Andrew Edis QC was appearing for the prosecution and Lord Carlile QC for the defence. Hazell was brought into the dock wearing black-rimmed glasses, a washed-out blue T-shirt and tracksuit bottoms.

At 2.05pm the jury of seven men and five women were sworn in. The prosecution said they intended to call 14 witnesses – 5 police officers, a pathologist, a shopkeeper, 4 prison officers and 3 expert witnesses. Opening for the prosecution, Andrew Edis QC, told the jury that he would begin with a 'navigation' of the murder.

'It is brought by the prosecution that Stuart Hazell

murdered Tia Sharp when she was 12-years-old,' Edis told the court. 'She was the granddaughter of Christine Bicknell, who he was having a relationship with at the time, making him her step-grandfather. It's an agreed fact that on Thursday, 3 August, she died a sudden and, we suggest, violent death at the home where Christine Bicknell and Stuart Hazell lived and where Tia would quite often come to stay. She had her own room there.'

He stated that they knew there were only two people in the house at the time and that it might be suggested that Tia had died by falling down stairs. The jury would have to decide whether Tia was murdered or had died in a mysterious accident.

Edis added that there would be evidence that would need to be put forward, which was obviously part of a case like this. They would find some of the evidence 'distressing'. The judge also warned, 'Cases like these can arouse emotion but you must set emotion aside.' He asked the jury to keep calm and remain rational.

'The prosecution case is that Stuart Hazell had a sexual attraction for Tia Sharp,' said Mr Edis. 'There was some form of sexual assault and that was the reason he killed her.'

Hazell had secretly filmed Tia to satisfy his sexual interest in the weeks before she was killed, the prosecution said. After subjecting her to a sexual assault and smothering her, he went to extensive lengths to hide the body, the court was told.

The jury heard that Hazell had repeatedly accessed paedophile images of prepubescent girls on his mobile phone. Police had also found two memory cards from Hazell's cameras, which contained a series of secret photographs and videos of Tia, including footage of her sleeping on 16, 17 and 21 July when she was staying at her grandmother's house just weeks before she went missing. And there were 11 still images of her sleeping.

Another covert video showed a naked Tia putting moisturiser on her legs.

'She appears to be being secretly filmed,' said Edis.

'What is he taking these clips for?' Mr Edis asked. 'Did she know she was being photographed or, on the other hand, did he have a sexual interest in young girls – and in her in particular?'

Hazell had tried to hide one of the memory sticks on the top of a door frame at his home and in the kitchen, the prosecution said. A memory card also appeared to have been hidden in an electricity-meter cupboard. They contained 'extensive pornography' featuring young girls, including 'Grade One' pornographic images of underage girls and two 'extreme images' featuring bestiality, the jury heard.

'There are also a number of professional-type pornographic photographs with young teenage girls wearing glasses while performing sexual acts,' said Edis.

It seemed that Hazell sought out girls on Google who had glasses and a pony tail, and looked like Tia.

The Internet history on Hazell's phone showed searches of a website that was popular with paedophiles. Searches included the phrases: 'naked little girlies', 'young, young girlies', 'schoolgirl nudes', 'underage photos', 'young girls nude', 'daddy daughter pictures', 'illegal underage incest pics', 'little girls with glasses' and 'violent forced rape'.

Hearing this, Tia's mother, Natalie Sharp, left the court

visibly distressed, shouting, 'I hope you rot in hell!' before she was helped out. She remained outside court when the jury was shown the last image taken by Hazell on his mobile phone – a picture he then copied to his camera and which was found stored on one of the memory cards. The photograph was of a naked prepubescent girl. The face cannot be seen but the prosecution maintained that it was Tia Sharp, lying on her bed at her grandmother's home after Hazell had killed her. There was blood visible on the bedding in the picture and, in the corner of the photograph, the hand of one of the girl's dolls could be seen. Relatives of Tia and two jurors sobbed after the image was shown. Others gasped as they wiped away the tears.

The court heard Tia had used BlackBerry messaging, or BBM, on her mobile phone to speak to a friend until 00:42 BST on 3 August. After that, the prosecution said, she did not use her mobile phone ever again.

Edis said it was reasonable to suggest that she had died after that time, and he told the court the photograph of her seemingly dead on the bed was taken between 3am and 6am on 3 August, the day she went missing.

'That is a picture of a dead, naked prepubescent girl on the bed. That's a picture of a dead girl on Tia's bed,' he said.

The prosecution maintained that a pathologist who had both examined the body and the photograph would say that the marks on Tia's body indicated that she had been 'posed' in the position seen in the photograph. Shot from behind, it showed her on all fours and leaning over a bed in an obviously sexual position: 'He [the pathologist] said the irregular mottling on buttock and back of thighs is suggestive that it may be a photograph of an individual taken in the post-mortem death and posed. That's the conclusion he reaches looking at the photograph.'

Edis then said that the doctor believed the body had been exposed sexually, which did not necessarily mean a sexual assault had resulted in death. But there was damning evidence to that effect.

'You know there is a dildo in his drawer with her blood on it,' he told the jury.

Only one conclusion could be drawn.

'The photograph... was taken in that house, that night, and taken, it would appear, as she was dead, by somebody who wanted to photograph her in that state for the purposes of sexual excitement,' Edis said, and he warned the jury that they would have to see the photograph again.

'You will have to see it because it matters,' he said. 'If it is a dead girl on Tia Sharp's bed, photographing her naked, its importance is obvious.'

The jury were given a ten-minute break due to the graphic nature of the evidence. But Hazell, in the dock, appeared unmoved.

The court heard that the duvet was bloodstained and that the DNA evidence showed that it was a billion to one against the blood coming from anyone other than Tia. Edis said that semen found on the bedding and Tia's nightclothes were from Hazell by similar odds of a billion to one. There was the same degree of certainty that the blood on a sex toy found in the bedroom that Hazell shared with Tia's grandmother also came from Tia.

Continuing, the prosecution said Hazell then claimed

that Tia had run away from home after he had gone to great lengths to hide her body and other incriminating items in the loft of Tia's grandmother's home. He wrapped the child's body in a sheet, before sealing it in a bin bag with sticky tape and hiding it in the attic.

'Christine Bicknell left the care home where she worked around quarter past two in the afternoon,' said Edis. 'She got home and later on they reported Tia missing. At that time, the defendant said he thought he had heard her saying she was meeting a male friend at The Whitgift Centre but he couldn't remember because he was doing house chores. He knew perfectly well where she was but wasn't talking to anyone.

'Police went to the house on the third, and on the fifth [of August]. Although police went into the loft, they didn't find the body because it had been meticulously wrapped and hidden. There wasn't any smell at that time.'

However, Edis told the jury that the police did eventually find Tia's body. 'They only found it, I am afraid, because it had started to smell,' he said. 'It was quite well hidden. It has been moved up and then across within the loft space.'

Edis told the jurors that they would hear the suggestion that Tia had died in an accident after falling down stairs and that Hazell had panicked and not known what to do.

'Accident had nothing to do with this, and one question you are going to have to ask yourself is, "If that's wrong, what was her blood doing on that dildo?"' said Edis. 'The probability of it being anyone else's is less than one in a billion.'

For the prosecution, then, the case was clear.

'We know when she died, we know where she died,' said Edis. 'We know this – there were only two of them in the house at the time. So was it murder or may it have been an accident? What we know is that, after she died, he put her into the loft – now that is not what you normally do with someone who has suffered an accident. Generally speaking, if someone has an accident and you are concerned about their health, you call an ambulance. That is not what happened here. He undoubtedly put her body in the loft in order to hide it.'

Hazell also stored another bin bag containing incriminating items in the loft, the prosecution said. The contents included his T-shirt, which was found to have the child's blood on it, jeans, a pair of trainers, her Umbro top and a pair of his spectacles, which were broken and carried one of Sharp's fingerprints on the lens. The jacket had traces of Hazell's DNA inside the collar and Tia's blood on the outside, it was said.

'The idea was to say that Tia Sharp had left home... this was the lie that was being prepared,' said Edis.

The court heard how, in the interview Hazell gave to ITV News, he appealed for Tia's safe return, insisting she was like his own child. She was his 'golden angel' and he did not know what had happened to her. 'He was playing the role of a bereaved grandparent who wanted nothing more than for her to come home,' said Mr Edis. 'He, of course, knew perfectly well where she was but wasn't telling anyone.'

The court was told that Hazell had planned, in due course, to remove the body from the house but was foiled because the area was 'besieged by the media'. Edis said,

'That was to be a terrible nuisance to Mr Hazell. Normally, he has the run of the house in the hours of darkness, quite often when Christine is at work. No doubt, when he put her in the loft, having wrapped her up as he had done, he expected there would be an opportunity for him to go back to the loft and take her somewhere else. But, of course, that wasn't possible with all the local people, the press and the police laying siege to the house.'

When her body was found in the loft a week later, the decomposition was so bad that it was impossible to ascertain the cause of death. However, Edis said a pathologist would tell the court that smothering was the most likely form of death.

Traces of Hazell's semen were found on a duvet cover and pillowcase recovered from Tia's room as well as her pyjamas and a pair of her floral boxer shorts, while Tia's blood was found on the bed covers and the belt Hazell was wearing when he was arrested.

Three days after Hazell had killed Tia – while her body was in the loft and the search was still going on – he had tried to access an incest sex website on his phone, Mr Edis said.

In Belmarsh prison in south-east London, the court was told, Hazell had spoken to a prison officer. 'He told the officer, "It wasn't sexual. I am not a nonce or a pervert,"' said Edis. 'He said he had been playing with her on the top of the stairs and she fell down and broke her neck.' However, Edis said, the pathologists were unable to find any evidence of a broken neck or skull fracture consistent with dying from a fall. His findings were consistent with suffocation.

Mr Edis continued to relate the story Hazell had told.

'He then took Tia upstairs to bed thinking she would "get better",' he said. After that, Hazell told the prison officer that he 'panicked and did not know what to do', so he put her body in the loft and covered it with a blanket. But, Edis said, 'the parcel containing the body… had been carefully wrapped – in a sheet first and then bin bags separately – in order to try and seal it using Sellotape. As you can imagine, that's not a particularly easy thing to do with a dead human being. But that's what had been done, no doubt to prevent any leakage. It was done for a purpose, a reason – something you may want to think about when you are talking about the panic.'

In a letter written to his father from prison, Hazell said, 'They are trying to say it was sexual but I promise you it wasn't. If I had a chance, I would end it here. I've got no money, no fags, no hope. It's the Hazell curse. I have only got myself to blame and that will stick with me until my time comes and that won't be long.'

Again, the jury were told that they would have to decide whether Hazell was guilty of murder, or whether Tia died by accident as he maintained.

'It is an agreed fact in this case that, on the night of Thursday, 2 August, and Friday, 3 August, she died a sudden and, we suggest, violent death at the home where Mr Hazell and Ms Bicknell lived. The issue in the end for you to decide will be this,' said Mr Edis. 'Has the evidence made you sure that Tia was murdered or do you think it may well have been an accident?'

Summing up, Edis said, 'Firstly, there is a dead girl in the loft. Second, there is an image of an apparently dead girl taken in that house that night at three or six in the morning or thereabouts and taken, it would appear, if she was dead, by someone who wanted to photograph her for the purposes of sexual excitement. She was injured in the photograph, hence the blood. We have the dildo with her blood. We have his semen and another semen stain from him on the floor. We have his interest in young girls for sexual purposes, demonstrated by photographs and web searches that I have referred to. We have his interest in Tia Sharp in particular, demonstrated by those photographs of her rubbing cream on her legs and sitting on a couch with her friend and taken of her while she was asleep. Remember her grandmother was not by any means always at home when she would stay at her house. The prosecution say that this is clearly no accident. The alternative theory involves falling down the stairs. Because of the delay in finding the body, pathology's identification was more difficult than it might have been. This was not an occasion they were able to say, "I know what the cause of death was," but many negative findings – no fractured skull or broken neck that would explain a fall.'

On the second day of the trial, Steven Carter was joined in the public gallery by 15 reporters from various newspapers and press agencies, while Stuart Hazell carried papers with him into the dock. Natalie Sharp arrived late.

Proceedings began with a recital of the agreed facts and the jury were taken through the schedule of phone calls and text messages sent on the night Tia Sharp died. The last text message that night from Stuart Hazell to Christine Bicknell was sent at 11.44pm. In it, he told her that he would call her the following day. The next morning Bicknell texted Hazell to say she would be home from work at 2.30pm.

Data taken from mobile-phone masts showed Tia's mobile being used at home at about 3pm on 2 August, then in Croydon from about 3.30pm. The prosecution said Hazell called Tia's phone hours after he killed her. The last outgoing call or text from Tia's phone was to her grandmother, Christine Bicknell, at 4.26pm on 2 August. And the last BlackBerry message was sent at 12.42am on 3 August. At 12.48 it disconnected from GPRS.

There was also a record of the texts exchanged between Tia and Hazell as he went to meet her in Croydon and the text where she asked to spend two nights at the house he shared with her grandmother.

The court heard that, during the journey from the station to the house, Bicknell texted Tia, telling her, 'Make sure you hoover under your bed. Love you xxx'. She later texted Hazell to say, 'There are two of you so you both can do all the housework.'

A statement from Christine Bicknell was read to the court by junior prosecutor Jocelyn Ledward. In it, she said, 'When Tia went missing, it didn't cross my mind that she could be dead. I always thought she was coming home. It didn't cross my mind that he would hurt her. He loved Tia, she idolised him. He absolutely adored all the grandkids and they loved him to pieces. They would kiss and cuddle him. I would have had to pin them down to get the same attention.'

She added, 'I love Stuart with all my heart, he was my world, but my granddaughter always came first.'

Hazell was not somebody she 'dragged in from the

street', she said. He worked as a window cleaner and was 'no ogre'. The couple had been in a relationship for five and a half years. She said she had first met Stuart Hazell in either 2002 or 2003 at the New Malden pub where she worked as a barmaid. She was not bothered by Stuart's previous relationship with her daughter Natalie. It had only lasted a few weeks. Bicknell and Hazell had got together in April 2007 and she admitted that Hazell was a drinker and smoked marijuana daily.

She said Hazell had known Tia since she was 'really really little' and all her grandchildren 'loved him to pieces'. She described Hazell as 'soft' with the children. The most he had ever done to discipline them was raise his voice. Bicknell herself said she had a strong bond with Tia and she saw her at least six days a week. It was not unusual for Tia to stay at her house, often asking Hazell before she asked her. Tia described her grandmother's house as a 'place of peace', though Tia and Natalie had a normal relationship. However, Tia had said that, when she was 16, she would move in with her grandmother.

In her statement, Bicknell said that on 1 August she had received a text from Tia asking if she could stay. She did not reply to this message because she knew she was working the following day. However, she texted Hazell about Tia's message, telling him it was his choice if Tia stayed. He would have to look after her, as she would be working until 10pm.

Hazell got in touch with Natalie and Tia and arranged to meet Tia in central Croydon. The next time Christine spoke to Tia she asked her to do some vacuum cleaning upstairs and Tia agreed.

Discussing Hazell's relationship with Tia, she said, 'The majority of the time he has her more than what I do... She is his cling-on.'

The court was told that Tia had texted Hazell the day before she went missing to ask, 'Stuart, can I stay at your house all weekend, please?' He replied, 'I will ask Nanny.' The message was accompanied with a smiley face and Tia texted back with a similar sign and wrote, 'OK, thanks.' The Old Bailey heard how Ms Bicknell had agreed to let Tia stay even though she would be working at a care home overnight, leaving Tia alone with Hazell. The next day, Mr Hazell went to Croydon to pick her up, where they were caught on CCTV.

'Tia was not the sort of girl you could groom,' Christine said in her statement. 'She was a mouthy 12-year-old – you couldn't force her to do anything. She is a mini-Natalie [Tia's mother], which is a mini-me.'

Bicknell said Hazell, who had previously dated Tia's mother, moved in with her a week after their relationship started in 2007. She said she had thought back over her relationship and had not noticed any particular changes in his behaviour, nor had any worries about Hazell being around Tia. However, she added that Hazell would occasionally get argumentative after drinking vodka but had been told not to drink it in the house. However, he would drink lager and smoke two joints of cannabis a day.

Bicknell said she got back home at around 2.30pm on 3 August. By then, the prosecution claimed, Tia had already been dead for several hours. 'I wanted to surprise Tia because she wasn't expecting me until about ten pm,' Bicknell said. 'When I got in, she wasn't there. Stuart was watching TV or on the PlayStation. I said to him, "Where's Tia ?" He told me she had gone to Croydon. She wanted to get a pair of flip–flops or sandals and he had told her to be back by six pm. He had given her his last tenner and I had a moan at him because that left us with two or three quid.'

She said Tia's phone was on charge, adding, 'He had tried to call her and he found it ringing at the back on the table. He said he hadn't realised she didn't take it with her because he was hoovering when she went out. I wasn't concerned about this. I thought it seemed accidental.'

Bicknell said that Hazell had told her that Tia was meeting someone in Croydon but that he did not know who as he was cleaning when she left. Bicknell said she then took a nap on the sofa. She woke at 6pm when Hazell said that dinner was ready. When Tia was still not home at 7.15pm, she became increasingly concerned.

As the evening wore on, concern turned to worry and she rang her daughter Natalie, Tia's mum. She had not heard from Tia either but suggested that she may have gone to a fair. Bicknell and Hazell then drove to Ashburton Park to look for Tia at the fairground. They searched the fair for about 45 minutes before returning home. Then Bicknell said she knocked on the doors of neighbours but no one had seen Tia.

Bicknell and Hazell then went to pick up Natalie from her home in Mitcham. They drove around searching for Tia. Finally, they drove to the police station in Croydon to report Tia missing.

Mr Edis said they reported Tia missing at 10pm on 3 August. A police officer said Natalie seemed genuinely worried when explaining the circumstances of Tia's disappearance. The officer also said he was given a passport-sized photo of Tia and was told she had no phone or Oyster card with her.

Returning home, Bicknell said she was sick with worry and thought Hazell was too. She said she looked at Tia's bed and it appeared as if it had been slept in.

Concerning the loft, Bicknell said she had never been in it. She said that Hazell had, although she had never seen him go up there. She'd felt sorry for Hazell, she said, as after Tia had gone missing, people were pointing the finger at him.

Before Hazell went missing, he told her he planned to go for an early morning walk before the press arrived. That night, she noticed a smell in her house and thought it was a cat's mess. When she woke that Friday, at about 9am, Stuart was not there, but he had left a note, which read, 'Back in a bit baby, went for a walk before press get here xxxx. Love you.'

She said she had not known what to think when he did not come back. She also said she had a good relationship with neighbours Paul Meehan and his wife Bobbie at number 21. She did not know why Meehan had, allegedly, lied about seeing Tia leave the house on 2 August.

Bicknell said that, when Tia went missing, it never crossed her mind that she was dead and Stuart hadn't told her anything about killing Tia.

The last images of Tia Sharp alive were shown to the court. CCTV caught her arriving at East Croydon railway station at 3.45pm on 2 August. She was wearing a yellow

T-shirt and blue leggings. Hazell, wearing a blue top and shorts, was seen entering the station shortly afterwards. The pair were then shown leaving the station and getting on a tram which took them to nearby Gravel Hill. After getting off at Gravel Hill, they were seen walking along a platform then walking past an Esso station in Selsdon Park Road, before spending 12 minutes shopping for groceries in a branch of the Co-op supermarket. After leaving, they looked in the window of a fish-and-chip shop. They were then seen on Tia's final journey, a T31 bus. They sat at the back before getting off at Fieldway, New Addington. In the last bit of footage, they are walking towards Hazell's home where Tia died.

Natalie Sharp sobbed as she viewed the footage of her daughter's last outing. However, the pictures looked innocent enough. In the company of Hazell, just hours before she died, Tia did not seem to have a care in the world. Christine Bicknell was sitting next to her daughter in the public gallery.

Phone records read to the jury confirmed Tia arranging to meet Hazell at a railway station in Croydon on 2 August. That evening the 12-year-old's grandmother Christine Bicknell spoke to Hazell on the phone and Tia could be heard laughing in the background as she watched TV.

Hazell had sent Miss Bicknell a text at 10.12pm saying, 'Tia's going to bed after *Family Guy* baby then I'm going to pass out.'

Bicknell replied, 'Ok… Tired and headache. Love you. See you tomorrow xxx.'

Another message from him at 11.44pm said, 'Night, night baby, call you tomorrow xxx.'

But the prosecution claimed that, instead of going to bed, he attacked Tia over the next few hours.

The court were told that there were two searches by police of the loft in the days after Tia vanished but officers failed to find the body. But the smell grew progressively worse. By 9 August, Bicknell had noticed a stench and told an officer, 'I'm very sorry, there's a terrible smell up there. One of the cats has shat somewhere and I can't find it.'

By this stage, she said, Hazell was 'in a daze and walking around aimlessly'.

A search on 10 August uncovered Tia's remains, the jury were told. Hearing this, Natalie Sharp put her head in her hands.

Bicknell said she had not suspected Hazell until Tia's body was found in the loft. 'I knew nothing about her death,' said Bicknell. 'If I knew, he could be dead – I would be inside because I would have killed him. I found out the same time as everybody else, that Friday. I didn't know anything.'

Bicknell said Hazell did not have access to the Internet and 'he wouldn't have a clue how to do it, so he says'.

She added, 'I have been asked by the police if Stuart watched or downloaded pornography to his phone. I have never seen him do anything like that.' She said she had found some images on his phone but he claimed they had downloaded accidentally, the court was told. She and Hazell had a digital camera but the memory card had been lost after she'd taken it to Asda to get pictures printed. Regarding the picture of Tia putting cream on her legs, Bicknell said, 'I did not take this film.'

After Tia had died, but before anyone realised she was missing, Hazell calmly prepared a meal for her and sent loving texts to her grandmother knowing, the prosecution claimed, that the girl he had murdered lay dead in the loft.

The court heard that Hazell told Bicknell that Tia had gone shopping. Bicknell told the court, 'I said, "Oh, where's Tia." It was a bit before six. Stuart said he had cooked our dinner and had some left for her. It was pizza and chips. He'd cooked the pizza but left the chips for her.'

A statement from Mark Williams, a colleague of Hazell's at the window-cleaning company, was then read out. In it, Williams described Hazell as 'not bright but heart in the right place'. Williams said he'd been surprised when Hazell had not turned up for work on the Friday Tia's body was found.

But according to his boss Adrian Van-Aalst, Hazell was a 'fantastic liar'. After Tia had disappeared, Van-Aalst said that Hazell had put his 'hand on heart' and sworn that he had nothing to do with it. He had also accused the media of tarring him as 'Jack the Ripper'.

Mr Van-Aalst also spoke of his shock at reading comments by Hazell's father Keith in the newspapers. 'I was surprised,' he said. 'Stuart had previously said his father was dead. He went into great detail about his father's death.' Hazell had told colleagues that his father had died of a heart attack. As a result, he had taken time off and even broken down in tears at work. In his statement, Van-Aalst said, 'If Stuart's dad isn't dead and this is not true, I would say he is a fantastic liar.'

After failing to turn up for work on 3 August, Hazell and Van-Aalst exchanged a series of text messages. On 5 August, Hazell texted, 'Still no news. This is f— nightmare come true.'

On 8 August, he texted Van-Aalst about the press who were camping outside his front door, claiming, 'B— are getting everything wrong, they are making me look like Jack the Ripper.' He added, 'Hand on heart mate, I don't know where she is. I wish I did. This is madness. I had nothing to do with this.'

Another of Hazell's work colleagues said that he'd phoned Hazell on Friday, 3 August, regarding work but Hazell's phone had been switched off. The following day he tried to contact him again. This time Hazell replied with a text saying his granddaughter was missing and he had been out searching. He asked Hazell whether he was the last person to see Tia and he replied, 'Nah, nah, nah, mate.'

Later Hazell texted him saying the press were getting everything wrong and, again, were making him look like Jack the Ripper. His colleague said he advised Stuart to say nothing to the press and to keep his face away from the cameras.

The Old Bailey was told that police officers – including a specialist search team – missed two chances to find Tia Sharp's body in the loft of her grandmother's house.

The space was first examined on 4 August, the day after Tia was reported missing. Sergeant Keith Lyons, who spent five minutes looking in the attic, said, 'I didn't move around the loft further as I would have to crawl. I was searching for a missing girl and the loft seemed very clear and I thought, "She's not hiding there." I felt it wasn't safe enough and I would fall through the roof.'

The loft was examined the next day during a search by a team of six specialist officers. PC Steve Jeffries spent 25 minutes looking in the roof space. He said, 'I positioned myself as best as I could to look around both sides of the tank. I couldn't see anything of interest.'

In a statement, PC Richardson said she was sent to New Addington to search Tia's room on Saturday, 4 August. She said police looked in Tia's bedroom where she found items of Tia's clothing including her school uniform. She also said that Hazell told her he had given Tia £10 to go to the shop to buy flip-flops. Richardson felt that Hazell was genuinely upset and he had said he blamed himself because he should have taken her to get shoes rather than just giving her the money. The police then spoke to Tia's best friend and a boyfriend called 'Magic'. The court were also told that, meanwhile, 82 people had turned up at Addington police station volunteering to help the police in their search of the local area. They were sent home and told to search outbuildings.

The statement continued, describing how another policeman who searched the house said he started at the top. When he saw the loft hatch, he asked for ladder but was given a chair instead. This was not high enough but the policeman managed to struggle into the loft by pressing his feet against the walls and pulling himself up. He then said he was surprised at how clear the loft was. There appeared to be nothing in it but a water tank with a wooden cover. He left the search at that because, at the time, he was looking for a live girl. 'I was searching for a missing girl,' he said. 'But, from what I saw of the loft, it was pretty clear. I thought, "She's not hiding in here."'

Another officer said that, two days later, he saw bin liners in the loft. He also held a torch for his colleague, who looked in the loft for two minutes. At the time Hazell was very quiet and calm and would occasionally look at him and nod. Yet another police officer who searched the loft on 5 August said he opened black bags that contained bedding but decided they were too light to be significant.

The police statements revealed still further incompetence. A police specialist search officer said he had had to ask colleagues where it was safe to walk in the loft because he had not searched one before. A dog could not be taken up there because the floor of the loft had not been boarded.

'The PC who searched the loft and a supervising sergeant were subsequently given words of advice,' said Commander Neil Basu in his statement. 'Both officers are devastated by their failure to find Tia and this case has deeply affected all those involved. The PC voluntarily decided to remove himself from search duties.'

The police also recorded that on Monday, 6 August, a handbag, make-up, clothing and shoes, all belonging to Tia Sharp, were seized from the room where she had been staying. And on 10 August further items were taken. These included a duvet from Tia's bed, a bottom sheet, a pillow, a onesie and a laptop.

The court was then told that the police returned to the New Addington home on 10 August to pick up a jacket belonging to Hazell. It was then that they noticed a bad smell. A police dog was called in. Later that day the house was cordoned off and a crime-scene manager was brought to the house to examine the loft. A large wrapped package was found there. It appeared dust free and 'body-shaped', the prosecutor said. The body was later formally identified as Tia Sharp. Again, at the testimony, Natalie Sharp held her head in her hands.

The crime-scene manager had been accompanied by Detective Constable Daniel Chatfield. He said that there had been a strong smell of decomposition when he entered the loft. The jury was shown a series of photographs of the loft. DC Chatfield said that they had been searching for about ten minutes when his colleague alerted him to what he thought was Tia Sharp's body. As DC Chatfield gave further evidence about the discovery of Tia's body, Natalie left the public gallery.

'The loft was extremely confined, it was very hot and quite chaotic,' he said, 'so there were a lot of boxes and bags around the hatch entrances, which needed to be moved in order to search further into the loft. After about ten minutes my colleague Mr Langley had alerted me to what he believed to be the body of Tia.'

He ripped open the bag, exposing a foot.

DC Chatfield searched the loft of the New Addington house again on 13 August to see if there were any other items that looked as though they had been recently placed there. He said that he found another black bin bag, which was photographed before being cut open. Inside there was a cardboard box containing two carrier bags, one from Tesco's one from the Co-op. Inside the Tesco bag he found a yellow top and light blue-grey trousers or leggings. At that point, Christine Bicknell fled from the public gallery sobbing loudly and the courtroom was cleared for a short break. Natalie and Christine did not return when the hearing resumed.

DC Chatfield told how a sweet or ice-cream wrapper was found inside some newspaper and a pair of broken glasses was found in the wrapper. Later Mr Edis said that Tia Sharp's fingerprint was found on the lens. The glasses were shown to the jury. Also inside a Tesco bag was another package – a white trainer wrapped up in newspaper.

Other officers found a memory card. As it appeared to be hidden, DC Chatfield had had a photograph taken of it. Another memory card was found on the door frame, and a digital camera, which was then shown to the jury, was found in a kitchen drawer.

Photographs of a large luggage strap hanging close to the loft hatch were shown to the jury. DC Chatfield said that a string was also found on one of the floor joists in the loft. Were these perhaps used to lift Tia's body up into the loft?

Lord Carlile then began his cross-examination for the defence. Asked about the search of the loft on 10 August, DC Chatfield said that there were a number of items between the loft hatch and Tia Sharp's body. That's why it had taken the crime scene manager around ten minutes to find it.

DC Chatfield also admitted that they had not been wearing forensic suits when they entered the house. However, these were donned downstairs before the search of the loft began. Lord Carlile then asked about normal police procedure and the possibility of contaminating the evidence. He was told that items that were seized were immediately separated to prevent contamination.

Carlile then asked about the sex toy found in a drawer.

Had DC Chatfield been told about it before it had been taken out of the drawer? 'When you lifted up the sex toy from the drawer, you had no idea what had happened to it [in the] previous seven days,' Carlile then said.

On the third day of the trial, the court heard testimony from four members of staff at Belmarsh prison. The first to be called was Paul Leahy. He said that Hazell's mood had been low when he arrived at Belmarsh on 13 August. Leahy told the jury that Hazell said, 'Since Friday I've been feeling guilty and I just want to kill myself.'

Hazell had also said he tried to get razors blades from his bag to cut his wrists while he was in custody at a police station.

According to Leahy, Hazell added, 'I have a real problem with my anger and, when people say wrong things to me, I can flip. I just feel like hurting everyone.'

Hazell had said he was a self-employed window cleaner and he regularly cleaned windows at Croydon police station. He also expressed concern about Tia's funeral on 6 September.

Two days before, on 4 September, Leahy said Hazell told him he wanted to talk about the case, although his barrister had told him not to. This was advice Hazell did not intend to follow. He told Leahy, 'It's been going round in my head and I keep having the same nightmare over and over.'

But Hazell also said that he could not sleep.

Leahy added that Hazell believed the police should investigate his neighbours and insisted he had been set up and that other people had seen Tia alive. 'He said that the police had fitted him up and he claimed that there were six people to see her after him,' Leahy said.

He told the guard that he believed neighbours could have moved Tia's body into the attic of the house he lived in as the buildings in the terrace had interconnecting roof spaces and he insisted that someone had deliberately put the body above his house. 'What the press don't tell you is that all six or eight houses have joint lofts,' Leahy said Hazell had told him. 'The police have searched my house four times and not found anything, with dogs and some specialist search teams. In my opinion, someone has moved her into my loft.'

He claimed he was a 'big bloke' and it was impossible for him to get up into the loft. Hazell then pointed the finger at Somali neighbours, describing them as 'bacons' – prison slang for sex offenders. Leahy said Hazell told him, 'They were shouting and throwing plates at each other. It's them the police should look at, they are the bacons, not me.'

Tia, Hazell said, had been the target of paedophiles who had been grooming her by contacting her on her phone. Leahy told the court, 'He claimed that Tia had paedophiles hassling her on her iPhone. Apparently, he was 25 years old but messaging her claiming he was 13. She used to bunk off school and he said he had gone to the woods to look for her because it was a place she liked to hang out. He had a photo of Tia and was asking people if they had seen her.'

Hazell told the prison officer, 'If I killed her, why would I be there? I would have done a runner to Scotland or Germany.'

Leahy told the court that the prison staff were concerned for Hazell's safety. They were not so much concerned about what other prisoners would do to him but more about what Hazell would do to himself.

In prison, Hazell was already beginning to change his story. After claiming that he was innocent and had nothing to do with Tia's death, he now began to say her death was an accident, and also told Prison Officer Warren Fegan, 'I'm not like Ian Huntley [the Soham murderer who killed Holly Wells and Jessica Chapman in 2003]. It was nothing sexual, I'm not a nonce.'

'He was saying that the press was trying to make it look like it was sexual but it wasn't,' Fegan continued. 'He was saying that he loved his step-children [sic]. He said that it was an accident; she had fallen down stairs and broken her neck. He said that he didn't know what to do and he picked her up and took her upstairs and laid her on the bed, and he thought that she would get better. He didn't know what to do, so he wrapped her in a sheet and put her in the loft.'

Fegan said Hazell was full of remorse and felt sorry and guilty.

'He asked me how hard it would be to prove not guilty to murder but guilty to manslaughter,' the prison officer told the court.

Fegan said that he carried out an Assessment, Care in Custody and Teamwork (ACCT) interview with Hazell when he arrived at Belmarsh prison on 13 August. The risk of him harming himself was judged 'at the far extreme'. Fegan said Stuart Hazell was 'very, very distressed' when he arrived at the prison. He kept saying he was 'sorry' and said he 'wanted to be dead'.

'He really wanted to kill himself,' Fegan said. 'He was saying he was sorry and he felt guilty. Initially, he feared for his personal safety. He was very, very distressed. He was clearly saying that, any opportunity he had, he would kill himself.'

The prison officer added, 'He wanted to be dead. He wanted away from everything.'

Prison Officer Fegan said that Hazell had talked to him again two days later.

'He stated that he wished he could turn back the clock.' Fegan then quoted Hazell saying, 'I deserve everything I get. If I get 25-30 years, I don't care – I deserve everything I get.'

Fegan then he asked Hazell how he felt. 'He held up one hand and said, "Guilty, guv,"' adding that he could not get the images of Tia that the police had shown him out of his head.

Jocelyn Ledward read a statement from senior prison officer Gerald King, who also said he was told by Hazell that Tia had died in an accident.

The statement read, 'He stated that he wanted to end it and take his life. He didn't want to be seen as an Ian Huntley. He added that it was an accident; that he had been playing with her at the top of the stairs as they always did. She fell down the stairs and broke her neck. He wished he could turn back time. He then laid her on the bed for a while, then wrapped her in a blanket and put her in the roof. He wanted to make sure that people knew that it wasn't a sexual thing.'

The court also heard a statement from prison officer Dan Dobson, who said Hazell had told him, 'It's bollocks, they've got nothing on me. The loft runs from one end of the street to the other. How come they searched it five times and found nothing?'

According to Dobson, Hazell told the senior prison officer he wished he had told Tia's family it was an accident. He said that the family were talking about revenge and what they would do to whoever had taken her or hurt her.

King said Hazell went on to say that he wished he had said Tia's death was an accident. 'He wished he had told them it was an accident,' said King, 'as he was with the family listening to what they would do to whoever had taken her or hurt her. And he was saying what he would do to this person as well.'

Hazell had further regrets. King went on, 'He wished that he had explained the accident to his partner but he didn't want to ruin the relationship.'

Prosecutor Jocelyn Ledward and Detective Constable Darrell Ayaydin then read a transcript of a police witness interview that Hazell had given on 5 August. In the interview, Hazell described meeting Tia in Croydon, the pair spending the evening together before she went to bed, and then her leaving to go to Croydon on her own the following morning. He told police she wanted to buy some sandals, but, as he hated shopping, he had given her some money and let her go alone. He also claimed that she mentioned going to meet a boy and spent the night before messaging someone, but he 'kicked himself' for not paying attention to the person's name.

Hazell said in the interview that there were no family arguments and that, if Tia had a problem at school, she would confide in her grandmother. He also talked of the journey he and Tia had taken from Croydon to New Addington on 2 August. He said he washed her clothes that night, that he was doing the washing anyway. He told officers it was not strange that he washed Tia's clothes. He said one item was marked: 'There was grass or mud or something on it.' He also said he and Christine Bicknell did not have a lot of money and did not want to waste washing powder.

Curiously, he also told the police that 12-year-old Tia did not drink. 'She did not touch a drop,' he said.

Hazell then told police they both did a bit of housework on 2 August in case her grandmother Christine Bicknell came home moaning – and that is why he gave Tia £10. He said Tia was on her BlackBerry phone all night and he told her she could either be on the phone or watch *Family Guy* on television. He said Tia went to bed after watching the cartoon sometime between 11.30pm and midnight. He had then woken up at about 7am the next day. Tia had set an alarm for 10.30am so she could get to Croydon. He recalled telling Tia to charge her phone and leave it on the side. He said he did not want to go Croydon, but told Tia she could go but that she had to be back by 6pm. Hazell said that Tia had some breakfast and was 'going on about going out to Croydon'.

He also told police that he did not recognise a lot of people who came to help search for her but knew they were family or friends. Then DC Ayaydin confirmed that Stuart Hazell was taken by police out of the house on 6 August so he could show the route he and Tia took from Croydon to New Addington.

After lunch, DC Ayaydin told the court there was an air of anticipation when he went to the property on 8

August, which was then surrounded by press. He and Hazell were mobbed by the media as they left the house to take Hazell to Croydon police station.

In the interview, Hazell said that he told Tia to be back for 6pm and that usually she was never late. In his second statement, he said, 'I swear to God she walked out of my house.'

He maintained that she had left the house on 3 August to go shopping and 'meet a boy from her old school'. Hazell told DC Ayaydin that he regretted not going with her and added, 'If I hadn't been such a lazy fucking bastard, none of this would have happened.' He went on to say that he kept her pizza-and-chips dinner in the oven for 'when she comes home'. The prosecution alleged that, by that time, she was already dead.

DC Darrell Ayaydin said, 'He said he was kicking himself for not going with her and said, "I hate myself every day for it. Anyone will tell you I love that girl to bits."'

He told the police that, when Tia went out at 12pm on the day he claimed she disappeared, he finished the cleaning and went on the PlayStation until her grandmother came home. On 8 August he had left Tia's dinner in the oven so she could have it when she got home.

Hazell's mobile phone, taken from him during the interview, was shown to the jury. DC Ayaydin said he took a different route to the house when dropping Hazell back after the interview, to avoid the press.

Hazell's defence lawyers began their cross-examination by saying that Hazell had showed agitation when he saw the media vehicles and, when he left the house, was asked provocative questions by the press. DC Ayaydin then admitted that the police had omitted to tell Tia's family not to wash her clothes and that her room was to remain undisturbed during the investigation.

The next witness was forensic pathologist Dr Ashley Fegan-Earl, who had carried out the post-mortem examination of Tia's body. The court was warned that his evidence could be upsetting.

The Home Office pathologist told the court that he'd been called by the police on 10 August after Tia's body was found. He said that the loft where Tia was discovered was self-contained and was not linked to neighbouring properties as Hazell maintained. He said that inside the loft he could see wrapped plastic sacking covered with a fitted sheet and it was clear to him that inside was a human body. It was obvious from the smell in the loft that the body was in a state of decomposition. The jury was then shown pictures of Tia's body in the bags. Fegan-Earl said he found no clear injury on the front or back of Tia's body during his examination.

He was then asked about the photograph of the naked girl found on one of Hazell's memory cards. Dr Fegan-Earl told a jury that, in his opinion, the person in the photograph was dead when it was taken. 'When I saw the photograph, there were changes in the body that suggested to me the individual was dead,' he said.

He told the jury it was 'irregular mottling' on the back of the thighs that made him come to this conclusion. It suggested the girl had been left lying on her back for some time after death before being moved. However, he said it was not possible to come to a definite conclusion about the cause of death. The Home Office pathologist told the court there was no clear bruising to Tia's neck and no sign of compression or strangulation.

'Considering the negative findings and exclusions, including the toxicology, and taking into account the case as a whole as presented to me, some form of suffocation or chest compression would appear to be the most likely cause of death,' he told the court. But, he added, as he could not be certain, the cause of death was formally recorded as 'unascertained'.

As far as Dr Fegan-Earl was concerned, Hazell's story of how Tia died did not hold water. He said there was no evidence to support a claim that she died after falling down stairs, as Hazell claimed. 'Throughout my examinations I could find no evidence of injuries that would suggest an accidental cause of death such as a fall,' he told the court.

When Tia's body was found wrapped in a black sheet, covered by plastic wrapping secured with tape, the court was told she was wearing pink-and-white pyjama bottoms, with a top that had the emblem 'Little Miss Giggles' on it and a bra, both of which were rucked up.

Dr Fegan-Earl said there were no visible signs of external injury. It was hot in the loft and decomposition had set in, so bruising or indications of suffocation would have been difficult to detect that long after death. There was no fracture of the neck, no bruising in that area and no damage to the spinal cord, he told the jury. He found no evidence of a brain haemorrhage, no evidence of compression of the neck, and none of her bones were broken. There was no evidence of natural disease that could have caused Tia's death. A fall down the stairs that could cause death would cause internal and external injuries, he said. Despite the decomposition, there were no cuts or gashes that suggested a fall, and there was no evidence of injuries that suggest accidental cause of death by a fall. Some form of suffocation or chest compression would appear to be the most likely cause of death.

Dr Fegan-Earl also said there was no pathological evidence of serious sexual assault. Hazell kept his head down and stared at the floor of the dock throughout this evidence being presented.

Hazell's defence put it to the pathologist that, if someone is being suffocated and they can fight back, material from the attacker would usually be found under the victim's fingernails. While Dr Fegan-Earl conceded that this had been true in past cases, none was found under Tia's fingernails. Dr Fegan-Earl was also questioned about how he came to his conclusions about there being no head injuries. The defence also argued that the photograph on the memory card could have been taken when the subject was alive.

The fourth day of the trial began with the jurors being read a statement by Dr Deborah Hodes, a paediatrician from University College, London. A child-abuse expert, Dr Hodes said that the photograph on the memory card found in Hazell's home showed a girl aged between 8 and 13.

A statement was read from Prasanna Jayakumar, the shopkeeper from Cannon Hill who served Hazell after the police had issued a warrant for his arrest. Hazell had bought a bottle of vodka and a lighter in her shop. She said, 'He looked tired and wasn't in a fit state. He looked emotional. He came up to the counter and asked for half a bottle of Glen's vodka and a lighter.'

She said he handed over £6.74. Before leaving the store, he told her his granddaughter was missing and, if she heard anything, to let him know.

'I said to him I was sorry to hear that and that I would help him if I heard anything,' she said. 'While he was saying this, he was knocking his hands against his head with both sides of his palms. It looked like he was struggling to cope. He mumbled [that] she hadn't been home to eat her dinner.'

Hazell left but returned.

'Two minutes later he came back for another half-bottle of Glen's vodka and a lighter,' she said. 'He held out his hand and I counted the money. He said he was looking for his granddaughter and wasn't going home without her. He left the shop and was stood outside speaking to passers-by.'

CCTV footage of Hazell in the shop was then shown in court. Another customer, a girl called Chloe, told Ms Jayakumar she had seen on television that a girl's body had been found in Hazell's home and that he was now wanted by the police. 'That's the man the police are looking for. It's been on Sky News that they have found the body,' Chloe said.

His photo had been on the television and she dialled 999.

This was followed by a statement by a Victoria Dragnet, who had been walking her dog and seen Hazell on Cannon Hill Common. She had gone there to look for a friend's missing dog. She asked Hazell if he had seen the dog: 'I took the opportunity to ask if he had seen a brown fluffy dog without a tail,' she said. 'He said, "I've got more important things to fucking do than look for a fucking dog. I'm trying to look for my grand-daughter. She's missing. I'm looking for Tia, Tia Sharp, the girl who is missing."'

Ms Dragnet said, 'I noticed his eyes were glassy. He looked as if he was off his face,' then added, 'He made me feel uncomfortable and I just wanted to get away from him. He said, "I can't just sit there. I need to find her."'

On her way back to her car, Ms Dragnet encountered Hazell again, when he apologised for being aggressive earlier. 'I really wasn't pleased to see him again. He gave me the creeps,' she said. 'Several times he said he was Tia's grandfather. He struck me as quite a volatile man but I listened to him and empathised with him… He seemed genuinely concerned. He looked flustered and he was in a tailspin.'

Ms Dragnet only realised who she had been speaking to when she saw Hazell's face on the news saying he was wanted in connection with Tia's death.

The court then heard that the police arrived and sealed off the area before searching the common where Hazell had been seen stumbling around and crying by dog walkers and sunbathers. A police dog tracked him to dense undergrowth. The police arrested Hazell on Cannon Hill Common as he emerged. When he was being arrested, he said, 'I don't understand. I'm her grandfather.'

Hazell was drunk – twice the legal drink-driving limit.

As he was taken away, a hostile crowd gathered, jeering and throwing insults at him.

In the police car taking him to Sutton police station, Hazell said, 'Murder? I don't believe it. I was only having a piss in the bushes. The police have got this all wrong.'

Hazell was examined in the police station. The court heard he had a black eye and said he'd been punched but would not say who by. Various bruises were found on his body, which he said were work related. During his interview, he made no comment and said nothing when he was charged later that night. The court was then told about the letter Hazell had written to his father, Keith Hazell, in Belmarsh. The full text of the letter, which had been intercepted, was shown to the jury. It had the word 'forgive me' written at the top alongside a sad face and read,

Dear Dad,

I know I am probably the last person you want to hear from but everything in the papers ain't true, they twist and make their own shit up. What happened I will explain in my time but put it this way it was an accident and I panicked, stupid I know but for my stupidity I am looking at 15–18 years. I regret it every second of every day and there's nothing I can do about it.

I think about taking my own life because if I don't someone will, that is a definite. I'm classed a Cat A prisoner, never thought this would ever happen, I hope your not getting agro because of me, you know I'm not the bad person everyone's saying.

I can't sleep can't eat I wish I could turn back the clock but I can't. I'm sorry to of [sic] lied to you all but I didn't know what to do. I understand if you rip this up and never want to know me again, I wouldn't blame you.

Christine got arrested, she had nothing to do with this. I loved her with all my heart and soul. God I hate myself. I should have gone about this a different way, told the police everything. They're trying to say it was sexual but I promise you that it wasn't. It was an accident and I was a prick to do what I done.

If I had the chance I would end it here and now, I got no money, no fags, no hope. It's the Hazell curse and I only got myself to blame and that will stick with me till my time comes which won't be long.

I just want you to know I love you all. I know Christine and family will never forgive me, I know what's coming and I deserve it.

I want to ask you one favour and one favour only. Send me a little bit of money in and I will never ask anything of you again. One mistake and my whole world has collapsed. My own fault I know but don't listen to papers like everyone else does. I will tell you in time.

I love you all, no doubt you will tell Sarah and Mark and kids I'm sorry, and mum Darren and family.

May god have mercy on my soul even though I don't deserve it.

Love always your son Stuart Xxx
I'm sorry truly truly sorry xxx :(
If you want a v.o [visiting order] let me know dad
with all your details. Xx

Forensic scientist Daniel Beaumont explained to the court how he identified blood. He explained that there was a chemical test that can be used to see if blood is present even if there is no clear stain. Then he explained DNA profiling.

Beaumont said that a small but heavy bloodstain had been found on a belt in Hazell's bag, by the buckle. The stain was strong though small, he told the jury. Both Hazell's and Tia's DNA were found on the belt. Beaumont said that there was a 'billion to one chance' that the blood did not belong to Tia.

Bloodstains were also found on a work jacket and a ring, which were also in Hazell's possession when he was arrested. However, no DNA profile was identified.

In his cross-examination, Lord Carlile used an example of a current news story in which Ed Miliband came to a cyclist's aid in order to question Beaumont's explanation of how to explain how Tia's DNA could have gotten onto Hazell's belt.

A broken bracelet belonging to Tia was also found in the kitchen of her grandmother's house in New Addington but Beaumont said it was impossible to say when it had been broken or whether it had been damaged accidentally.

The jury was told that Hazell's fingerprints were found on the bin liners and plastic bags containing Tia's clothes and the trainers found next to her in the loft. Beaumont said that fingerprints found on one of the plastic bags and the left lens of a pair of broken glasses also stashed up there matched Tia's.

Forensic scientist Frederic Boll was then called to the stand to give evidence. He had been called to the house in The Lindens after Tia's body was found. He discovered bloodstains, hairs, fibres and semen. He also examined cups to see who had been drinking from them.

Boll explained that chemicals are used to test an area to see if semen is present. The reagent reacts to an enzyme found in semen. Two areas of semen staining were found on the floor of Tia's bedroom. One had no DNA profile; the other matched Hazell's DNA.

Boll detailed the ways semen could have ended up on the floor. He also said that he had searched the house for signs of bloodstaining. Bloodstains were found on a mattress and on the loft hatch but neither yielded a DNA profile.

Boll was also asked about bloodstains found on Tia's Umbro top found in the loft, while jurors were shown pictures of it. It showed 'extensive areas of bloodstaining', which, Boll said, had been transferred through contact rather than being airborne. He also said that, judging by the shape of the stain, the blood had been wet when the T-shirt was folded. Boll had also examined some broken glass but no bloodstains had been found on the shards.

The defence counsel then cross-examined Boll about some white paint on the Umbro T-shirt. Some of the paint was clearly on top of the bloodstains but Boll could not say exactly when the bloodstain or the paint had got on to the T-shirt.

Evidence about the websites Hazell had browsed from his mobile phone was then introduced. The first search he made was to look for a weather forecast. The second used Google to search for 'images XXX'. Other searches carried out were for 'school girl nude XXX', 'naked little girlies XXX', 'young young girlies XXX', 'naked lil glasses XXX' and 'glasses very young XXX'. These searches were all made in June and August 2012.

The prosecution moved on to the memory card found in the hallway cupboard. Some images on it were of adult pornography; others showed child pornography, they said. The memory card also had videos of Tia Sharp sleeping and images of her sitting on the sofa. The jurors were told that some of the images had been deleted but had been recovered. However, many were small and of low quality.

The court was then shown images and videos recovered from the card. Three video clips showed Tia sleeping. One image of her sleeping had the embedded date of April 2009. The court was then adjourned for the weekend.

CHAPTER TWELVE

GUILTY!

The beginning of the fifth day of the trial at the Old Bailey was delayed. Then finally, when the court assembled at 11.06am on 13 May 2013, Lord Carlile, leading for the defence, asked for the indictment to be put to the defendant again. Hazell leaned forward in the dock, clutching his hands before him and hanging his head. This time, after a brief pause, he pleaded guilty.

Gasps and sobs could be heard around the oak-lined courtroom as Stuart Hazell admitted killing his partner's granddaughter Tia Sharp. Tia's natural father Steven Carter was seen crying. Someone shouted, 'Chicken.' It was plain from evidence the prosecution had presented the previous week that Hazell would not have been able to put up much of a defence.

Lord Carlile then spoke for Hazell, telling the court, 'He wanted it to be known that he thinks Tia's family have suffered enough. He does not want to put them through any further stage of this process.'

The jurors were then asked to formally find Hazell guilty.

The court was adjourned until 12 noon for sentencing. When the hearing resumed at 12.09, Lord Carlile told Mr Justice Nicol about a report into Hazell's background that he had submitted.

The jury then reassembled to hear any remaining details of the case. The prosecutor, Mr Edis, then told them that he had further evidence that would have been presented, which showed that Hazell regularly visited the websites of paedophiles. Another expert on DNA would also have given evidence. By then the jury's job was done. They could have left the court but all 12 stayed on to hear the rest of the trial.

Mr Edis went on to say that this trial fell into a small category of exceptionally serious murder cases and outlined the sentencing guidelines for the murder of a child, giving examples of sentences given in different cases.

The murder conviction in this case, he said, was more serious than most as Hazell had sexually assaulted Tia with a sex toy, and Mr Edis reminded the court that the pathologist had said that the blood found on bedding was either the result of a sexual assault or asphyxiation: 'She wasn't stabbed or shot,' said Mr Edis. 'She had no wound that the pathologist could find. The two explanations for the blood were blood from her nose or ears during the asphyxiation, or blood caused by the sexual assault.'

The change of plea meant that Hazell denied himself the opportunity to present his defence in court. He had no chance to explain himself, which meant that a certain amount of mystery still hung around the case.

'We do not know, and never will know, exactly what took place in the house in The Lindens that night,' said Mr Edis. 'But it is clear Hazell committed a serious sexual offence against her, killed her, took that photograph as some sort of keepsake then, in quite a calculated way, wrapped up the body and hid it in the loft.'

Speaking of the sexual assault, he added, 'What else it may have involved cannot be known.'

Mr Edis specifically drew attention to Hazell's behaviour in the taking of the photograph after she had died for sexual gratification. 'And having done that, in dressing her in her pyjamas and wrapping up separately her outdoor clothing and putting her body in the loft. This was concealment that lasted a week. That was carefully organised. He went on television to proclaim his innocence and, in the event, continued to deny what had happened even when he was arrested after the body had started to smell in the house.'

Despite Hazell's guilty plea, her family still did not know for sure how he killed her, or why, and the prisoner had not sought to enlighten them.

A victim impact statement from Tia's mum Natalie Sharp was read out in court:

> I grew up in a very close family. I had a special relationship with my Nan, my mum's mum. When I knew that I was expecting Tia, I was so happy that I would have something to love.
>
> Tia's father Steven disappeared before she was born

and I realised that the unique relationship I had with my nanny would be repeated with Tia and my mum. I did try to keep Tia in her father's life but, when he had a new family, it was obvious to Tia that he didn't want to know. So there was always me, Mum, my brother and Tia. A small but really close family unit.

My parents gave me a good childhood. They were together until 1999 and at the time they broke up I was angry. When Tia came along, I had a reason to keep out of trouble; if it had not been for her, my life would have been very different. She was mine and no one else's and I had someone to love.

When I was told Tia had gone missing, I always believed that she would come back. At the very worst, I thought I'd have to face the fact that someone had touched her and scared her and hurt her. I never really considered that she would be dead. How could I? Worse still was the false hope from the hoaxer[s] who said they had her. I thought she was coming back. Since Tia was taken, I have lost my trust in everyone. It is too hard for me to believe that she is really gone. I try to think of her as being on a sleepover at her friend's house.

Jack, my eldest son, who is three, asked me just this week if Tia was coming home from school soon. I've had to tell him the truth. It made him really cry. I told him that Tia is a star in the sky and now, when we go up to say goodnight, we look out of the bedroom window and speak to the star, the one that was bought in Tia's name.

I breathe for my children. I fear anyone hurting my

boys. I fear that if anyone touches my sons or does anything to them, what I might do, I am so scared and angry. I have been so badly hurt by people I don't know and who know nothing of me.

People have said the most terrible things about me as a mother and Tia's life. I can't understand how people who know nothing about somebody can send such awful messages. Then the other day a cabbie just asked me, 'How is everything going?' He apologised and said, 'I expect everybody asks you.' I realised he was the first person to ask me to my face without condemning me behind my back. I've been stared at and physically attacked and I know people judge me when they see me buying something nice for my sons.

My close family are closer still but this has hurt them so badly. My brother is struggling to work, my mum was suspended from her job when Stuart was arrested. I've heard people saying Tia was mistreated and that she's lucky to be away from this world. My Tia wanted for nothing. I have gone without so many times to give my children everything and the truth is that strangers have said things that have been repeated in the press and social media that have been unbelievable.

Tia was my mum's life. She was as close to my mum as I'd been to my nan. We'd all lived together when Tia was a baby and she was my mum's 'mini-me'. Tia loved to be with my mum. Wherever my mum worked, Tia was taken there to meet everyone. I sometimes felt a little green-eyed about their relationship but I could see it was like the relationship I'd had with my Nan – it was so unique and special.

I can't say what'll happen after the trial. It's my last hurdle. I haven't allowed myself to grieve yet; I need to finish this first. When the trial is done, everything is over for everyone else, but it won't be for us. At the moment Tia is still talked about. After this we still have to live with the next hurdles. Will Stuart appeal, will he get parole, will he be out and about in a few years?

I gave the ultimate trust to Stuart. I have so much I want to ask him. Sometimes I feel pity but I want to hurt him, but I could never manage to hurt him like he hurt me. I want to meet him and I want him to answer my questions. Sometimes I think I would like to do this but I doubt the authorities would allow it.

This was followed by Tia's dad Steven Carter's victim impact statement:

The murder of my daughter Tia has shattered mine and my family's hearts. We will never get our heads around what has happened to Tia. My daughter Tia's life has been taken from us all, as we will never get the opportunity to share her 13th, 16th, 18th or 21st birthdays. We will never have the chance to see Tia walk down the aisle and get married and have children of her own. We have all lost someone special.

The love for Tia will always be with us, our

memories of Tia smiling and playing will never be forgotten. My last memory of Tia is her jumping into my arms, giving me a kiss and her telling me she loved me. I will never get this opportunity again, but it is one of the many memories I will cherish for the rest of my life.

All my family and friends have their special memories, the community of New Addington have lost someone special and they themselves will never forget Tia. Myself and those of my family with children will never be the same as we have all stopped our children's freedom to go out and play as we fear of something happening.

Myself, my partner, my son and members of my family are suffering from post-traumatic stress. This has caused me to lose my temper quickly, have sleepless nights, cold sweats and generally be unhappy.

The court then heard that Hazell had a long roster of previous convictions that included disorderly behaviour, racially aggravated common assault, burglary, theft, criminal damage, grievous bodily harm, possession of marijuana and dealing drugs. There were 30 criminal convictions in all, resulting in 3 prison sentences. In February 2010 he was jailed for 12 months after being convicted of having a machete in a public place, and in 2002 he was jailed for 28 days for aggravated common assault, followed by 34 months for selling crack cocaine.

Stuart Hazell's record showed that he was a career criminal. He had followed in the footsteps of his father Keith Hazell, who was recidivist with convictions for theft, burglary, firearms offences and damage to property. Hazell dismissed his chequered past as the 'Hazell curse'. However, nothing in his background suggested that he was a paedophile capable of murder. He had no previous convictions for sexual offences.

When Tia went missing, Hazell had tried to bluff his way through.

'My previous has got nothing to do with it,' he had said. 'Everyone's got a shady past. That's ten years ago, for God's sake. Did I do anything to Tia? No, I bloody didn't. I'd never think of that. I know deep down in my heart that Tia walked out of my house. I know she was seen walking down the pathway. She made her way down that track. What happened after that I don't know.'

It was all a pack of lies.

Wearing a T-shirt emblazoned with Tia's face and sitting in front of a missing-persons poster of her, Hazell had told the world, 'It's not about me, it's all about Tia and we've got to get her home. I just don't know what more to do.' He looked into the camera and made a direct appeal to Tia, saying, 'Tia, come home, babe.'

All the time, he knew she had never left and, while volunteers combed the surrounding streets and woodlands, he'd known where she was.

After lunch, it was noted that Hazell had already spent 272 days in jail on remand. Lord Carlile pointed out that making submissions on behalf of someone in Hazell's position was one of the more challenging parts of his craft. It is 'one of the hardest things we have to do... but also one of the most important,' he said.

Nobody who had heard, watched or read about the

trial could feel anything other than sympathy for the family of Tia Sharp. As Carlile said, there was no greater loss for a family than the loss of a child just about to enter her prime.

'We do not seek to reduce or trivialise the seriousness of this crime,' said Carlile. Hazell knew he was going to spend decades in prison. However, Carlile added that 'he did not embark to kill for sexual or sadistic motivation. He did not set out to kill her at the start of that evening...'

Lord Carlile said he also wanted to make it clear that Hazell did not plead guilty on the basis he set out to obtain sexual gratification from the killing of Tia. It was not absolutely clear whether the graphic photograph believed to be of Tia was taken after her death.

The background of the case was detailed in Tia's grandmother's statement, he said. In it, she emphasised the strength of the relationship between Tia and Hazell. If there had been any history of sexual misconduct by Hazell towards Tia, Christine Bicknell would surely have noticed it. There was no evidence of any sexual grooming or activity towards Tia by Hazell before the attack.

However, detectives believed Hazell had removed the bathroom door in Tia's grandmother's home so that he could spy on the schoolgirl. He was also thought to have modified the light socket in her room to create a 'spyhole' in order to watch her.

'We know Hazell had a sexual interest in young girls and girls in glasses from his web browsing,' said Carlile. 'But Tia was happy being around him... One of the sad truths in this case is that he probably did love Tia and certainly did love Christine. And he will have to bear for the rest of his life what he has done to the woman who was probably the only person in his life that he has really loved.'

Making videos of Tia sleeping and moisturising her legs falls short of grooming, Lord Carlile said, and he dismissed Hazell's long criminal record as a roster of 'petty convictions'. True, he said, Hazell had known Tia since she was a toddler but he had become increasingly obsessed by her as she reached puberty. Throughout July and early August 2012 he filmed her sleeping, zooming in on her face, captured her as she put cream on her legs and, a day before he killed her, took numerous pictures of Tia as she sat chatting with a school friend at her mother's house in Mitcham.

Psychiatrists had already studied Hazell and recorded his psychological history. On that basis, they had attempted a diagnosis of his character and personality. Their report said Hazell had little contact with his biological parents. His father was in prison and his mum was working as a prostitute, and Hazell had been placed in care as a young age. He began drinking at the age of 13 and became dependent on alcohol. His first conviction came a year later. By this time he was homeless, abusing solvents and cannabis, and claimed he was sexually assaulted in a hostel in Soho.

According to Lord Carlile, 'Hazell, who inveigled his way into the Sharp family after first establishing a relationship with Tia's mother and then moving in with her maternal grandmother, was the product of an abusive upbringing – but denied the killing had a sexual motivation. Hazell, the son of a prostitute, received his first conviction aged 14 and was taken into care at a young age. He claims to have been raped while living in a homeless hostel at the age of 16.'

Hazell had psychiatric history of depression, self-harm and suicide attempts. Many of his problems had been caused by drugs and alcohol. However, his life had changed when he met Christine Bicknell.

'She provided the first stability in his life,' Lord Carlile said.

While reports said Hazell's borderline-personality traits were a result of his neglectful childhood, Lord Carlile said this did not excuse his behaviour and that Hazell would return to prison, where he would be marked out as a vulnerable prisoner. There he would be at serious risk of violence.

In mitigation, Lord Carlile went on to say that Hazell was a man 'who has an extraordinary capacity for living through lies that he has made up. The easiest thing for Stuart Hazell to do would have been to brazen out the rest of this case, possibly, or not to give evidence. His decision to plead guilty today is probably the bravest decision he's ever made in his life. Perhaps the only brave decision.' The defence maintained that it was a 'first act of remorse'. Throughout these submissions, Hazell sat with his head hung in shame.

Once the defence submissions were over, the prosecution returned to the issue of the damning photograph of a little naked girl. Mr Edis addressed the date and time recorded by the camera, which was understood to be incorrect. Earlier photographs were actually taken in July 2012, although the camera said they were taken in April 2009.

The prosecution argued that Hazell should get at least

30 years in prison without parole. Mr Edis told the court that Hazell could face a whole life sentence if the murder of Tia Sharp was sexually motivated.

Lord Carlile then said that Hazell had accepted he would spend 'decades and decades' in jail. During that time, he would be in 'constant danger', he said. 'There can be no doubt that in the aftermath of this case every adjective of vilification will be used about Mr Hazell. As a result, he will return to prison today as a marked and vulnerable prisoner.'

Every day of his sentence would be a 'severe punishment' for him, Carlile added, again insisting that there had been no pre-meditation on Hazell's part, nor any sexual or sadistic motivation. However, there was no doubt that his conviction was correct. 'Of course he accepts that, whatever happened that night, he killed her with the requisite intention to justify a conviction for murder,' said Carlile. But any sexual activity, he said, took place 'very near to the end of Tia's life'.

At 3.14pm, the judge adjourned the trial, saying it would reconvene for sentencing at 10.30am the following morning. Outside the court, Steven Carter said that a sentence of 30 years would not be harsh enough. 'I'm glad that Stuart Hazell changed his plea to guilty this morning,' he told waiting reporters. 'The four days of trial here were very hard to deal with, hearing the vile things Hazell did to Tia. Hazell will be sentenced tomorrow. In my opinion, it will not be enough. He should serve his time and be hung [sic]. I do not see today's events as justice for Tia – merely a legal conviction. I would now ask to be left alone so I can grieve and put my life back together.'

When asked on television whether she thought a 30-year sentence would be adequate, Natalie Sharp replied, 'Yeah, more I want him to rot in jail, I want him to stay there for ever and ever and ever – get what's coming to him.'

Senior investigation officer DCI Nick Scola said,

The conviction today of Stuart Hazell for the murder of 12-year-old Tia Sharp in August 2012 will, I hope, bring some closure for her family, who have seen justice served. However, Hazell's conviction will never bring Tia back and her family will have to live with her loss for the rest of their lives.

Tia was murdered by a man who had gained the trust of Tia's family and who, on that day, was tasked with looking after her whilst her grandmother was at work. Hazell abused that position of trust by planning an assault on Tia that ultimately led to her murder.

The evidence was overwhelming and clearly Hazell realised he had no choice but to plead guilty. However, he put Tia's family through a week of heart-breaking evidence in court and I wish, for their sakes, he had admitted his guilt sooner. Hazell is an extremely dangerous individual who poses a significant threat to young girls and it is only right that he should be imprisoned and removed from society so that he can no longer pose any risk.

I would like to pay tribute to Tia's family for showing such courage and stamina throughout this horrendous ordeal – from the time of the murder through to the conviction – and I truly hope they can move forward with their lives in the knowledge that Hazell will now pay for his crime.

DCI Scola reiterated Scotland Yard's apology to Tia Sharp's family outside the Old Bailey for not finding Tia's body sooner. But he said that, while finding the body during the first two searches would have meant Hazell would have been arrested and charged sooner, it 'would not have made any difference to what happened afterwards, merely brought it forward'. The police would still have had to deal with Hazell's lies and investigate his interest in child pornography and young girls.

'The early searches were really just a look round, they were not deep searches,' he added.

The Metropolitan Police also issued a statement regarding their failure to find Tia's body until the third search of the loft at her grandmother's home. Commander Neil Basu said,

Local officers visited the address on the night she was reported missing [3 August].

As is routine in missing-person cases, this was an initial visit to assess the situation and briefly examine the property. It was not intended or considered to be a full search of the property.

On the evening of Saturday, 4 August, two police sergeants and two PCs from the local borough checked the rooms, loft space, outbuildings and two vehicles at the address as part of the missing-person investigation. The officers involved were not specialist search officers.

Another search was held in the early hours of Sunday 5 August. This involved a team of specially trained officers, consisting of one police sergeant and five PCs.

They were briefed to look for evidence that could help find the 12-year-old. The search strategy included checking rooms that Tia had access to within the address. The loft was checked but a systematic search was not carried out.

Officers visited the property for a fourth time on Wednesday, 8 August. A search dog attended to sniff areas that hadn't been searched before and were less accessible, such as under floorboards and bath panels. The dog did not go into the loft – it had been searched before and was not boarded out (and therefore not accessible by the dog).

Due to the length of time Tia had now been missing and an odour detected inside the property, a decision was made to conduct an intrusive search of the property on Friday, 10 August. It was then that her body was found, well concealed in the loft.

The MPS immediately launched a review of the searches that had taken place and, in particular, the loft search.

This review concluded that human error around how the search was both conducted and supervised was primarily to blame for Tia's body not being found, rather than broader organisational failings, although the inexperience of the PC who searched the loft was also a contributing factor.

The PC who searched the loft and a supervising sergeant were subsequently given words of advice.

Both officers are devastated by their failure to find Tia and this case has deeply affected all those involved. The PC voluntarily decided to remove himself from search duties.

The MPS [Metropolitan Police Service] apologised to Tia's family as soon as it became apparent that her body had been missed.

While the police failure did not contribute to Tia's death, the MPS deeply regrets that this error caused additional distress to Tia's family by prolonging the situation when it could have been brought to an earlier conclusion.

Commander Basu added that the selection process for search officers would be standardised.

DCI Scola explained the effect that the failure to find the body earlier had on the investigation: 'When the body wasn't found on that significant search, what it meant was the whole investigative strategy was undermined to an extent because the baseline was that Tia was not in that house. So all lines of enquiry going on from that point had to look at where she might be.'

Alison Saunders, Chief Crown Prosecutor for London, added 'This was an appalling and unthinkable crime, made worse by Hazell's efforts to hide Tia's body and disrupt the police investigation. As an adult and trusted family member, he had responsibility for ensuring Tia's safety. Instead, he abused and murdered her. We recognise that this is an extremely distressing time of the family and I would like to pay tribute to them for their strength and fortitude throughout this case. I hope that this prosecution and the result can provide them with some small crumb of comfort in what has been a terrible time for them.'

Grandmother Angie Niles spoke of her relief after Hazell changed his plea to guilty. She told the *Daily Mail*, 'Obviously, it's a very emotional time for all of the family who are sitting here around the TV, but in a strange way we also feel relief. It says a lot about the man, just when you thought he couldn't do any more to our family he's dragged this out over months insisting he was innocent and only now at the very last moment has he put his hands up and admitted what he has done.'

However, she felt that, in some way, it was good that he hadn't admitted his guilt straight away. 'In a strange way I feel like it had to happen this way – maybe it's good that a judge and members of the public have had the chance to hear exactly what this sick man has done,' she said. 'Maybe it's good for all of us to have heard the truth in court so that none of this was buried, none of this remains secret.'

Now, Mrs Niles thought, the family could feel some sort of relief: 'It does feel like some sort of closure, it feels like it was the right time,' she said. 'Now we can get on with grieving for my beloved granddaughter. The process isn't easy but now we can get on as best as we can. I hope the judge locks him up for ever and throws away the key. He doesn't deserve any more than that.'

For Natalie, however, there remained unanswered questions. 'Once, you accept what has happened and you try to come to terms with that, you just want to be able to grieve for your child,' she said. 'But we haven't been able to mourn. There's so much I don't know and, as a parent, I'm supposed to know. I don't know if she was scared, I don't know if she suffered – I don't know if my baby suffered before she died. That's the worst.'

However, Natalie drew comfort from the fact that her daughter was mature and independent for her age, and would not have given up her life easily: 'If I know one thing now though, it's this: Tia was a fighter. Whatever happened to her, it wouldn't have happened without a struggle. She could look after herself. She used to look after her friends – none of them were bullied when Tia was around; she knew to stand up when something was wrong. So the one thing I do know is that, whatever happened, she stood up for herself.' And Tia's fingerprint, which was found on the lens of Hazell's broken glasses in the loft, showed that she did fight back when he suffocated her.

On Tuesday, 14 May 2013, just 24 hours after Hazell's dramatic guilty plea, he was handed down a mandatory life sentence. The minimum tariff he must serve is 38 years. That means that he would be at least 75 before he is even considered for release on licence. There were cries of 'beast' from the public gallery and Christine Bicknell could be seen crying and hugging a relative.

Passing sentence, the judge Mr Justice Nicol told Hazell, 'Tia was a sparky girl, full of life. You took that life from her. All that lay ahead of her – a career, loves and family of her own – will now never be. And the loss of her has been devastating for her mother, her father and all her relatives and friends. The tragedy of their loss and her death is because of your act in murdering Tia Sharp. You are responsible.'

Hazell's last-minute change of heart did not seem to have impressed the judge. 'Your guilty plea has come very late,' he said. 'It follows a wholly fictitious account of Tia falling down stairs and breaking her neck.' Concealing the body in the attic had meant that Tia's family suffered the agony of uncertainty as to what had happened to her. 'And time after time, you spun the wholly false story that Tia had left home on Friday morning and just disappeared,' the judge added.

There were, however, some mitigating circumstances, which the judge mentioned. 'You had an unhappy childhood,' he said. 'You had very little contact with your mother and you were placed in care when you were very young. You have a psychiatric history of depression, self-harm and suicide attempts. A consultant psychiatrist considers you fulfil the criteria for Unsocialised Conduct Disorder. Your poor coping strategies led you to drugs and alcohol. None of these matters is an excuse for what you did to Tia.'

However, the judge also said that there was no doubt Hazell had developed a sexual interest in Tia. 'The records of your Internet searching on your mobile phone make abundantly clear that you were looking out for pornographic pictures of pre-teen girls, which Tia was; pornographic pictures of girls who wore glasses, which Tia did; even pictures involving incest,' he said. 'Tia was not your blood relation but there was the bond between you because of your relationship with Christine and, from time to time, you referred to yourself as Tia's grandfather. You took pictures of Tia while she was asleep. In other contexts they would have been of no interest but your Internet activity included searches for pornographic pictures of young girls sleeping.'

Nevertheless, there was 'no pathological evidence' that she had been sexually assaulted, although this could not be discounted. 'I cannot say for certain that there was a sexual motive for the killing,' the judge added. Shame and fear may also have been a motivating factor, he said. 'It is not a case where a whole life tariff can be imposed.'

The judge said that, in such a case, a minimum tariff of 30 years was the baseline. However, there were a number of aggravating factors in this case which were both 'notable and serious'. These included Tia's young age, his viewing of paedophile pornography online, the 'gross breach of trust' exhibited by Hazell, and his concealment of her body. Mr Justice Nicol also said the picture of Tia, taken when she was naked and probably dead, 'further degraded' the young girl. While pathologists believed that the picture had been taken after she had been killed, the judge said he had to be sure that her murder was sexually motivated before he could impose a whole life tariff. And it could not be proven up to criminal standard that the photograph was taken after she died.

'It is an aggravating feature that your victim was so young,' the judge continued. 'So, too, is your abuse of trust. Tia's mother allowed her to come and stay with you because she trusted you to look after her. Christine was at work that night, she trusted you to look after her. By first sexually assaulting and then killing Tia, you betrayed that trust in the most grievous way possible. And that breach of trust reverberates still. Tia's mother has spoken of how she now finds it hard to trust other people in many other ways. I have said that I cannot be sure that the photograph of Tia was taken after her death but, whenever the picture was taken, it shows that, beyond the sexual assault itself, you further degraded that young girl by photographing her in such a dreadful position.'

Of the picture itself, he said, 'Her face is not visible but it must be Tia. Your counsel accepts that the only sensible conclusion which I can draw is that there was sexual conduct of some kind between you and Tia at some point.'

Hazell had changed his plea to guilty very late in the day. The judge told him, 'Your counsel says that you wished to avoid causing further distress to Tia's family. That is very commendable but they have had to endure four days of a very public trial. The prosecution had to deal with the account of Tia's death which you gave to prison officers and your father – a wholly fictitious account of Tia falling down stairs and dying as a result of an accident. And so it was necessary for the prosecution to lay out for the jury your sexual interest in Tia and for the jury to see the photograph of Tia naked. Your plea of guilty has spared the family none of that. It may be the first act of remorse, as your counsel says, but because it comes so late, I am afraid it will earn you only the most modest of credit.'

Hazell leaned forward, staring intently, then bowed his head while the judge passed sentence. Cries of 'yes' were heard from Tia's family as Hazell was taken down from the dock, taking with him the secret of how he killed Tia to his prison cell. The family left the Old Bailey without speaking to the reporters outside, although some of Tia's relatives shouted 'nowhere near long enough' and 'RIP Tia' as they walked passed journalists.

DCI Scola, who had led the investigation, said he was 'very pleased' with the sentence handed down to Hazell. 'A minimum of 38 years is satisfying for both the investigating team and Tia's friends and family,' he said. 'Hazell will have a very long time in prison to think about what he has done… Thirty-eight years is the longest sentence for any case I have investigated, the same for many of my colleagues. Hazell's 37 years old now. Add the 38 years on. He will be at least 75 before he comes out of prison.'

Chief Superintendent David Musker, Borough Commander of Croydon Police, said, 'This is a deeply tragic case and I would like to express my sincere condolences to Tia's family and the wider community of New Addington and Fieldway. Stuart Hazell has rightly been convicted of this heinous crime on overwhelming evidence. I would like to thank all those in the local community who have supported and assisted Tia's family and the police to bring about this successful prosecution. Justice has been done. I would ask the local community for calm and sober reflection to honour Tia's memory.'

However, Tia's father Steven Carter was far from satisfied by the sentence.

'It's no justice for Tia,' he said, clenching his fist. 'Justice would be if she were still alive.'

His father also said that the jail term was 'not really long enough'.

Hugging a friend outside the court, Natalie Sharp was

asked whether she was pleased with the sentence. She merely shook her head and left in a taxi without further comment.

Later she told the *Sun* that 38 years was 'not enough'. By comparison, Soham murderer Ian Huntley was given life with a 40-year tariff. Natalie also expressed the hope that other prisoners would inflict rough justice.

'I hope the other inmates go after him. I want him to live in fear for the rest of his days,' she said. However, she had been told that for the first three weeks of his sentence Hazell would be held in the 'vulnerable-persons unit' of Belmarsh maximum-security prison, where he would be watched around the clock by guards who feared he was a marked man. The other inmates were said to be gunning for him as a 'nonce'.

The father of one prisoner said, 'Some have nothing to lose because they are never getting out. Why not have a go at him? When they do, he will be ripped apart. Even though he is segregated, he can be got at. He has legal visits when he has to talk to his lawyer. That means going over into another part of the prison where the regular inmates are. That is when they will do him.'

Outside the Old Bailey, Christine Bicknell said, 'When I heard the judge say 38 years, I turned to my family and said, "We've done it." Then I broke down. Someone shouted, "Beast!" and there was a very tense atmosphere. I'm still a bit numb but I know this is as near as we'll get to an ending. I didn't sleep a wink last night. Everything kept swirling around my head again.'

Then in a more reflective moment, she said, 'We just wanted justice for Tia. But even now I don't really know if there is such a thing. How can anything make amends for what Tia suffered or for our life sentence? Tia isn't coming back to us, so the only thing that matters is that Stuart dies behind bars after suffering a living hell.'

The judge's talk of Hazell's sexual motive had unsettled her. 'He talked about that photo of Tia's body and the degrading things Stuart had done to her. I can't bear the thought [that] that photo exists. It's the final humiliation for our poor girl.'

Later, Natalie said that the circus surrounding the trial had made it impossible to grieve and that she remembered Tia as a lively, bubbly child − 'a typical 12-year-old, I suppose'. She took people saying that she was not a fit mother with a pinch of salt. It was 'water off a duck's back', she said. 'People are going to have their opinions. We're all guilty of that. I've opened newspapers before and read things and assumed… What can I say? They don't know nothing [sic]. She was loved. She never went without.'

But elsewhere, Natalie revealed she had been very upset by people she did not know passing judgement. 'I've been judged as a person, I've been judged as a mum, I've been judged as scum,' she said. 'I've been judged in every way I turn. But yet nobody knows, no one knows the truth. They don't give you the chance for the truth. They just listen to what they have heard and that's it − that's a fact.'

Natalie said that what had happened had made her relationship with her own mother stronger. She had no idea that Hazell had a violent streak. It had never come to the fore before. 'He was like two different people,' she said. 'The person I thought we knew, he was soft, gentle, friendly, there wasn't an inch of bad bone in him…'

Not knowing why Hazell had killed Tia was torturing her, she said. 'Even if I did know, I don't think it would change the fact that he had done it, but part of me needs to know why.'

The criminologist and child-protection expert Mark Williams-Thomas who had interviewed Hazell back in August gave his own view: 'Having met him, you would not say this guy's a killer,' he said. 'And the family were very clearly saying – whatever people were saying from the outside about his horrific offence – there was no sign, no indication to say that this was a man who was going to go on and kill. What he has put the family through by not pleading guilty at the earliest opportunity... because everything was out in court. Every single detail came out in court. And that's what's really upsetting.'

When he had interviewed Hazell in August, he was still denying the murder. But Williams-Thomas hadn't believed him. 'That's why I went to interview him because I knew that there could only be one person and that person was him,' he said. 'He was the last person to see her. But I interviewed him in such as way that, hopefully, it was going to help the investigation.'

Williams-Thomas has spent a lot of time with the family and he admired them. 'I think their dignity, the way they have held themselves all through it is a credit to them and a massive, massive credit to Tia,' he said.

The failure of the police to find the body earlier had also been an aggravating factor. 'Knowing Tia was dead was one thing,' he said. 'Knowing Tia was dead and in a loft in the house that they were in is beyond words.'

Step-father David Niles said that he still could not

believe what Hazell had done. He was 'part of the family', he said. Niles explained that he was waiting until their two boys were a little older to try and explain properly what had happened to their older sister. Hazell had a good relationship with Tia, he said. He would not have imagined that Hazell could have hurt Tia – 'not in a million years', he said.

'I had known him for seven years and he seemed all right to me,' he said. Niles had never thought there was anything dodgy about him and he didn't suspect anything until Hazell went missing the day Tia's body was found. Now the whole family wanted him to rot in jail and never come out.

Meanwhile, *Sun* columnist Rod Liddle said, 'Hazell was a cowardly, depraved and sadistic imbecile – and there are a few like him, lurking on the underside of society, down among the real dregs. People who do not know the concept of right and wrong, or who are so weak-willed that they are not able to resist even the most monstrous of actions. His sentence seems to me about right – 38 years before a chance of parole. Unless some other criminal gets to him inside. Some tough-nut villain who likes to feel better about himself because, even though he might be a total scumbag, he's not quite on the same corrupt level as Hazell.'

However, readers echoed the sentiments of David Niles and wrote in demanding that Hazell be left to rot in jail.

CHAPTER THIRTEEN

REVULSION

On the day that Stuart Hazell changed his plea, his sister Vikki Bartlett told the *Sun* that the family had disowned him as a monster. 'I hope he rots in jail,' said the 28-year-old.

And she issued a heartfelt apology to Tia's family, 'I feel terrible for Tia's mother. I've got two children. I cannot contemplate what she is feeling. If I could do something to bring Tia back, I would.' She never wanted to see the twisted killer again, she said. 'I don't want to know him – he's sick. I wish he was dead.'

There was no love lost between brother and sister. 'Stuart is nothing to do with me these days,' she continued. 'I don't want to be associated with him. I hate him.' And her mother Sharon felt the same: 'My mum never wants anything to do with him again,' said Vikki. 'She's gone through enough and it's not her fault.' She continued, 'I don't even think I can apologise for him because he's nothing to do with me – but I would like Tia's family to know that me and my mum are very sorry.'

The family had long been estranged. 'When we were young, he robbed my mum. She has disowned him. He was a waste of space and I hope he dies in prison.'

The final straw had come when they learned of his hideous addiction to images of the sexual abuse of children. 'We can't stand him,' said Vikki. 'Mum never wanted anything to do with Stuart. She was devastated when the news broke that he was arrested – she didn't want anyone to know it's anything to do with her… When he's on, I've turned the TV off. I didn't want to see him. I didn't go to court because I'd probably kill him myself.'

Her judgement on her brother? 'He's a thief, he's a junkie and he's a dirty man.'

However, elsewhere it was reported that Hazell's closest family had stood by him, and that his sister and dad Keith had been regular visitors at Belmarsh. No doubt the evidence presented in court had changed their minds.

After Hazell pleaded guilty, Natalie Sharp still had questions she wanted answered. 'I want to visit him in prison,' she said. 'I want to look him in the face and ask, "Why did you hurt my little Tia?" She was a harmless little girl who couldn't hurt a fly. I wish I could kill him with my own hands.' Tia, she added, had had ambitions to become an actress.

To Natalie, the thought that her daughter's body was in the loft while she slept in the family home below remained upsetting. 'How could she be up there and I did not know?' she said. 'I'm still sick now when I think about it. I slept right underneath her all that time.'

And, of course, Hazell had also put the family through five days of hell with his charade at the Old Bailey, before suddenly pleading guilty. 'He says he did it to spare the family more grief,' said Natalie. 'What more hurt could he do than make us see that picture time and time again?'

Despite Hazell's insistence that he was 'no Ian Huntley', Natalie believed that he was a monster along the lines of the Soham killer. 'He's just as bad as Ian Huntley,' she said. 'He's the most vile creature on this planet. I just hope the prison won't let him kill himself. My Tia is in heaven. I want him to stay in hell on earth with me... Hanging or lethal injection will never be enough. He should be made to suffer more. Instead, he will get three meals a day, he gets his rights. He doesn't deserve it... I despise him. I just want to see him beaten and brought back to life and then beaten unconscious again.' She was relieved that Hazell wasn't given any reduction in his sentence for his last-minute guilty plea.

As she had had a brief affair with Hazell before he had turned to her mother, Natalie was racked with guilt for the part she had played in letting Tia fall into his clutches. 'I blame myself,' she told the *Sun*. 'I should have seen something. I should have stopped Hazell.'

But no one had suspected him.

'I trusted him 100 per cent,' said Natalie. 'He had looked after my toddler son the weekend before. Tia loved Hazell. She couldn't wait to spend time with him. She was a mini-me and had a big mouth like me. I'll never have any more children because there's no way I can replace her.'

Natalie recalled the last time she had seen her daughter. 'She came up to me and gave me a squeeze and a cuddle as she left. 'She said, "I love you," and I told her, "I love you back and I'll see you Monday." I'd give anything to have one of those cuddles again.'

She was also critical of the trial procedures that resulted in the horrific photograph of her daughter being shown: 'It made me sick,' she said. 'Nobody needed to see that.' It was, however, judged to be a vital piece of evidence that the jurors had to see. But Natalie said she could see it too from the public gallery. 'People sitting around me could see it,' she said. 'How do you think having that picture on display to everyone in court makes us, her loved ones, feel? Awful. That shouldn't have been allowed. Did it really help justice? I don't think so.'

The offending photograph was viewed three times. It was first shown to jurors on TV screens on the opening day. That alone caused visible distress to two of the women on the panel. However, members of the public, including Tia's family, also caught a glimpse of the picture when it was reflected from a window. Many gasped in shock and Natalie fled from the courtroom in tears.

The trial was moved to another courtroom in an effort to restrict any further accidental viewings of the photograph, which was displayed twice more in the following days. On those occasions, it could still be seen by many in the court, including journalists and police. However, as already mentioned, Mr Justice Nicol had drawn attention to the importance of the photography when sentencing Hazell.

After Hazell's arrest, Tia's mum and her partner David Niles had moved out of their council flat in Mitcham as they could not face going into her room again. Hazell's conviction should have heralded a new start. Instead, she said, 'We will never move forward again.'

Tia's dad Steven was unequivocal. He wanted Hazell dead: 'I'd like him to pay the ultimate price but I'm hoping he'll suffer every single day in jail. He's a child-murdering nonce. I wish I was in jail to give him what he deserves. He should be in no doubt I'll be waiting for him when he comes out.'

After the trial, the police released new footage of Hazell refusing to answer their questions over the murder of Tia on 11 August. During the interview, the convicted drug dealer kept his head down and stared fixedly at the table.

When asked, 'So what can you tell me about the murder of Tia Sharp, Stuart?' Hazell remained silent. Then after ten seconds an officer prompted him again, saying, 'Stuart?'

Then Hazell became agitated. He began twitching and scratching his head. Still avoiding the gaze of the officer seated opposite him, he mumbled, 'Can I have a couple of minutes with my solicitor, please?'

That was as much as they could get out of him.

Christine Bicknell told the *Daily Mirror* of her revulsion that she had been 'cuddled and comforted' by the killer when Tia's body was in the loft above their heads. But she had no idea that, for five and a half years, she had been 'living with a monster'. She, too, felt that she had failed Tia after being taken in by the man she called her 'soul mate'. Her whole world had fallen apart, she said, after she realised that he had snuffed out the little girl's life and left her body in the stifling loft to rot.

'I let my baby down and I will never be able to get over that,' Christine said. 'I spent five nights in that house being cuddled and comforted by the man I loved, praying for Tia to come home safely. Her mum, Natalie, even came round and stayed with us because we were holding each other together. But all the time, Tia's body was above our heads, all alone wrapped in bin bags... and Stuart had killed her.'

Like Natalie, she blamed herself. 'But I didn't know, why the hell didn't I know she was there?' she said. 'I'm her grandmother, I should have protected her but I failed her... I blame myself. I should have seen something. I should have stopped Hazell. I despise him. How could she be up there and I did not know? I'm still sick now when I think about it. I slept right beneath her all that time.' Christine felt that the one person Tia should have been able to count on was her. 'All her life I'd told her she could rely on me, that I'd look after her.'

And like other concerned adults, Christine had briefed Tia on the dangers lurking outside the home. 'I'd warned her about all the evil people out there, the paedophiles and sickos, and had the stranger-danger chats. But all the time the danger was in my own home and I had absolutely no idea.'

People asked why she had not picked up the clues.

'Surely I must have suspected something... he was my partner, we shared a bed, we shared everything for five and a half years. But I swear, there were no clues that I was living with a monster.'

Now that the love she had for her treacherous partner was long gone, she, too, compared him to Ian Huntley. 'I feel nothing but pure hatred for Stuart Hazell,' she said. She cannot forgive him for the lies he told, or the four-day ordeal he put the family through in the courts. And she took issue with Lord Carlile, who said that Hazell changed his plea because the family had suffered enough and he did not want to put them through any further stages of this trial or this process.

This made her angry.

'He changed his plea to guilty, saying he was doing it to spare the family from any more suffering,' Christine said. 'That's sick and pathetic. He's the cause of all our suffering and we had to sit through four days of the most agonising evidence in that courtroom.'

'The worst part was everyone else hearing it,' said Natalie. She had hoped for a guilty plea on the first day so nobody would have to hear anything.

'Now I just want him to suffer,' said Christine, 'to go through the hell he has sentenced us to. Every day for the rest of his miserable life I want him to suffer mentally, physically, emotionally, to feel real pain. I won't ever have a chance of peace until he's dead and even then it might be too late for me. There can never be closure for us.'

As already seen, initially, Christine had seemed very composed when she came outdoors to help search for her missing granddaughter, but after the discovery of Tia's body, she lost much of her composure. She had been seen to cry, wring her hands and shake physically when recalling the sickening details of the family's nightmare. Her life had been torn apart by betrayal and loss.

'I want the chance to tell people what really happened,' she said. 'If there's one thing I could say to Tia now, it's, "I'm so, so sorry."'

The grandmother of five told the *Daily Mirror* how had

she had become involved with the window cleaner with a history of drugs and petty crime.

'I met him in Raynes Park Tavern in 2002 when I was working as a barmaid,' she recalled. 'His dad Keith was a regular, and I met Stuart through him. I knew Stuart had been in prison before, but I took him as I found him. He seemed like a nice guy, quite charming, funny... and I don't judge. We got friendly and he seemed to look out for me, care about me.'

He had had a brief relationship with her daughter Natalie, who also frequented the pub, before he spent time in prison. 'They weren't lovers, as far as I know,' said Christine. 'They were just friends.' The relationship was never an issue to the twice-divorced Christine and it was only in April 2007 that Christine and Stuart finally got together after weeks of phone calls and texts.

'He seemed like the perfect guy,' she said. 'He was affectionate, great with the kids, good around the house with the housework. He wasn't good in the bedroom. He never seemed interested in sex. But I loved him with all my heart.'

Christine said that she could not remember a single rocky moment in their five-and-a-half-year relationship before Tia went missing. Hazell's grandmother, Ruby Tilley, said she thought 'Christine wore the trousers' in the relationship. After Mrs Tilley sent him a Christmas card one time, Bicknell had confiscated the money from it, she said.

It was said that Christine was the only woman Hazell had ever loved. Nevertheless, she did have problems with Hazell's consumption of drink and drugs. He smoked at least two joints a day. 'He'd drink cans of Fosters and vodka and get very argumentative,' Christine Bicknell said. 'And he used to smoke weed as well in front of Tia and the other grandchildren. I used to hate that. I used to tell him, "No, not in front of Tia, you know I don't like it." But he'd carry on anyway.'

Despite what has happened, Christine still insisted that Tia and Hazell enjoyed a close and loving relationship. 'I could just tell from Tia's behaviour that she adored him,' she said. 'It was his choice to let Tia call him granddad.'

And Christine was certain that Hazell had not had any previous sexual contact with Tia. She would have known about it. 'If Stuart had ever tried any sexual advances on her, she would have said so. She'd have given him hell and come to me,' she said. 'If I had suspected for one moment he had so much as touched Tia, I would have taken a knife and killed him.'

She had told police that, if she had known anything, Tia would be alive, Hazel would be dead and she would have gone to prison. As it was, she remained convinced nothing had ever happened of that nature until the night he killed her.

'It was a one-off thing, I'm sure. And that's not me trying to assuage my guilt,' she said. 'He treated Tia like his own grandchild. How could I ever have known what he was really thinking?'

However, what he was really thinking had become all too apparent in the Old Bailey. Hazell, the man she had loved and trusted, had posed Tia's naked body on her bed in a scene of utter depravity, and the image tormented Christine. 'I have to fight, really fight to get that image out of my head,' she said. 'It has been seared into my brain and it haunts me.'

Each night as she tried to get to sleep, the sickening image filled Christine's mind and she shook and sweated. As an antidote, she kept a photo of Tia smiling at her bedside: 'When those horrible images flood in, I look at it and force myself to remember my lovely, lovely girl – smiling and full of life.'

But this was not always effective. 'Sometimes it doesn't work and I never get to sleep,' she said. 'So I get up and wander around talking to Tia. I speak to her every day. I tell her what we're all doing, say I hope she's all right and tell her how much I love her.'

Worse still, Christine had first seen Hazell's depraved picture of Tia under the most distressing of circumstances. 'When I was still under suspicion of involvement in Tia's death, I went back to the police station to answer my bail,' she recalled. 'I was sitting in an interview room when the police suddenly put a lot of images in front of me. It took a second to register what I was seeing… pictures of children, sick porn images. I didn't understand why they were showing them to me.'

Only later did the significance dawn on her.

'Then there was one photo of a naked body,' she said. 'I later found out it was the dead body of a young girl… now they say that girl was my Tia.'

The whole scenario was a terrible shock. 'I honestly don't remember what went through my head at that moment,' she said. All she remembers is feeling numb, in shock and a state of utter disbelief. 'From the moment I was arrested I felt I was fighting for my life and for Tia's memory,' she said. 'They thought I was guilty – or at least complicit.'

She had lost faith in the golden principle of English common law – that you are innocent until you are proven guilty. For four months Christine had had to endure being suspected of the most dreadful crime against her own flesh and blood. 'People were threatening to kill me on Facebook,' she said, 'and I was warned not to go to Tia's funeral.'

People assumed there was no smoke without fire and some had compared her to Rosemary West who, with her husband Fred, had killed at least ten girls after sexually abusing them. Fortunately, Natalie and David Niles never doubted Christine. They had been taken in by Hazell and his Mr Nice Guy act just as much as she had.

'They should give him a bloody Oscar for that,' she said. 'Now all Natalie has left are her memories of Tia – and her ashes. She keeps them in a box in her bedroom, surrounded by family photos and Tia's favourite belongings, and gives the box a polish every day. You might call it a shrine but that doesn't sound right. It's too sombre for a 12-year-old who loved life and all things pink and fluffy and fun.'

Christine also has the heartbreak of knowing that, apart from Hazell, she was probably the last person to hear her granddaughter's voice. It was the cheeky giggle she heard in the background when she'd called her partner's mobile phone, just hours before he murdered her.

'I was doing a night shift at the care home where I work,' she said. 'I rang Stuart on his mobile just to check if everything was OK at home as he was looking after

Tia. He answered straight away and said, "We're fine, I'm just playing PlayStation." Then I could hear Tia in the background.'

Tia had shouted down the phone, 'No, Nan, *we're* playing PlayStation.' Then they'd had a bit of banter about who was doing what.

'It was the last time I heard her speak and she sounded so happy,' she added.

In the morning, after killing Tia and hiding her body, Hazell had sent a text message to Christine saying, 'Morning baby just got up xx.' Later he texted, 'Text when you're on your way, I'll run you a bath.' Christine returned home from her night shift the following morning and went straight to sleep – blissfully unaware that Tia's dead body had been meticulously wrapped in a sheet and bin bags and was stuffed in the attic. At the time, Hazell had been waiting for any opportunity to move it and dispose of it elsewhere. The opportunity never came.

'When I got up in the afternoon, Stuart made me dinner and I sat down to watch TV,' said Christine. 'Just channel surfing. Then I realised it was six pm, and Tia still hadn't come home.'

As night drew on, Christine had started to panic. She and Hazell left the house and they drove around the streets looking for Tia. By that time, Christine was in a very emotional state. 'It was such a blur,' she said. 'I was driving all over the place.'

All the time they were searching, Hazell knew where Tia was – and that she would never be seen alive again. 'It chills my blood to think of how he was acting that night,' said Christine. 'He was completely calm. Even though he had just killed my granddaughter in cold blood, he played the part like a pro. Even to me, it appeared like he was genuinely searching for Tia.'

As the search continued, they found nothing and eventually contacted the police. Already Christine had begun to fear the worst for Tia. She was convinced from the beginning that Tia was no runaway. 'I just didn't believe she would have got on a tram to Croydon and run away from home,' she said.

When it became irrefutable that Tia was missing, Christine was in no doubt that her independent granddaughter must have been abducted. But she thought her abductor was a stranger. Christine was still convinced by Hazell's story.

'Stuart had said she had gone to Croydon to buy flip-flops,' she said. 'We let her travel on her own in the same way that you let a 12-year-old get the bus to school on their own. We just prayed she would be released unharmed and come back to us.'

Christine said she barely ate or slept all the time Tia was missing. Hazell was her rock, she said. Not only did the murderer make an effort to comfort her, a startling transformation came over his behaviour. 'I was also amazed that he stopped drinking and smoking weed,' she said. 'I thought it was because he wanted to be clear headed. How wrong could I be?'

Plainly, by then he had to watch every footstep, perhaps hoping that he would still have an opportunity to move the body. He had to be careful of every word he said. Soon he would face a police interview. Meanwhile, he let suspicion continue to fall on Christine.

When told that a body had been found in her house, Christine Bicknell still did not twig. She said she thought, 'Who is it?'

'I never dreamed it could be Tia,' she said. 'I always thought she was coming home. Always. I did not know how she was coming home but she was coming home.'

Gradually, it sunk in that the body was Tia's. Asked whether, at that point, she thought Hazell had killed her, she said, 'Most probably but everything is just jumbled into one at the moment. My head's just going round and round. I don't know what I am thinking now. I don't know what I thought then.'

By then Hazell had gone missing and Christine found herself being arrested on suspicion of murder. 'I can't remember if I was shouting, screaming, swearing or crying,' she said. 'I probably was – but I told them, "It wasn't me, I haven't done anything." No one believed me for months.'

Even after Hazell was arrested, some people still thought she knew more than she let on. 'But God knows, and Tia knows, I had no idea,' she said. 'I thought, I believed, she was in one of the safest places with one of the safest people that would ever protect her.'

When it comes to Hazell, she said, nothing would ever be enough. 'The best I can hope for is that he lives every day with the sheer hell we are living. And I hope that he suffers every physical, mental and verbal bit of pain that you can possibly give to one person. I really do.' And although the death of Tia and her shattered relationship with Hazell blights her life, Christine is all too aware that Natalie suffers even more than she does and is determined to spend the rest of her life supporting her, she told the *Mirror*.

The *Daily Mirror* claimed credit for exposing some of the inconsistencies in Hazell's story, allowing the police to build a case against him. DCI Scola said the information passed to him by the newspaper three days after Tia went missing had fuelled their suspicions. Hazell had told police Tia disappeared after leaving the home he shared with her grandmother Christine to go shopping. He said he was vacuuming at time, so did not hear her say goodbye. But he had told a different story to his family, who *Mirror* journalists had interviewed. They passed on the discrepancies, which had given detectives extra ammunition when they were questioning Hazell about the murder two days later.

'He told me he walked her to the tram station and waved her off,' his father Keith Hazell had told the *Mirror*. 'He said he would have gone into town with her but the tram was busy and he knew it would be busy in town. He said he didn't wait around to see her get on the tram.'

'Any information that comes to us like this that highlights inconsistencies is useful and always of value,' said DCI Scola.

Hazell had repeated his story that he was vacuuming when Tia left during the TV interview that took place two days before Tia's body was found. By then the police had been alerted to the inconsistencies in Hazell's story and DCI Scola said, at the time, detectives looked on the information supplied by the *Mirror* with 'great interest'. Hazell was charged with murder two days later.

Tia's uncle, David Sharp, also admitted that he'd been

taken in by Hazell. 'Now we know he was a monster but we all thought he wouldn't hurt a fly,' he said. 'He played with the children; he was great with them. But paedophiles can live right next door to you and you never know it. We just didn't know he could be capable of this. We still can't believe it.'

Since living with David's mother Christine, Hazell had betrayed nothing of his former behaviour and gave the family no reason to be suspicious, he said. 'He kept himself to himself. He didn't go around causing trouble; he wasn't out fighting or anything like that. That's how he convinced us all. People who do that don't do it overnight... so who knows what he's been up to before.'

Now he sees things in a different light: 'It seems that it was always his intention to do this,' Sharp told the *Daily Mirror*. 'Five years he's been close to the family. You've got to have some kind of background towards doing that kind of stuff in your life. You don't just wake up one day and think I'm gonna do what he's done to a 12-year-old child.'

However, at the time, on a Facebook page dedicated to finding Tia, David wrote, 'Stuart has done nothing wrong. The police are doing their job, he's got to make a formal statement. That's all, so stop pointing your fingers.'

He described how the family were still struggling to come to terms with the tissue of lies Hazell had spun when they were searching for Tia. 'He must have convinced himself he hadn't done anything wrong,' said Sharp. 'I don't know how else he could have sat with us in front of TV cameras and police telling all those lies. We knew he had been in prison for drugs ten years ago but that was in the past. We trusted him. He was amazing with the children. He could get down to their level. He was their granddad.'

Steven Carter, who had travelled down from Northampton for the trial, spoke of his shock at the guilty plea. 'When we arrived back in London on Sunday night, we were fully expecting to go a full week of horrible images and heart-breaking evidence,' he said. 'Then we went into court and saw a commotion with his legal team and they were running around before the start of the trial and we were a little bit worried. We had no idea. As far as we knew, it was to get some evidence blocked.'

Instead, the judge addressed the court, and Tia's family suddenly realised that Hazell was going to admit his guilt.

'I went cold all over,' said Tia's father. 'I just felt cold and the hairs on my body stood up. When he pleaded guilty, it was anger as well as relief. I feel he has taken the coward's way out. After all we have suffered, he put us through that last week and then he made out he had a conscience.'

That was not true as far as he was concerned: Hazell was just a coward. 'I just think he didn't want to stand in the dock and be questioned,' said Carter.

He had hardly known Hazell before the trial. 'I only met him once,' Carter said. 'That was on the first night when Tia was reported missing. I went to the house after going to the local police station. He came out and he put his hand on my shoulder.'

Then they had to relive the horror at the trial. 'It has been horrific,' he said. 'I am relieved for Tia that we don't have to hear any more evidence and see any more of these images. It is heartbreaking for us all as a family. Hopefully, my daughter can now finally rest in peace.'

Hazell was insistent that he did not want to be compared to Ian Huntley but the parallels with the Soham murders ten years earlier are striking. On Sunday, 4 August 2002, best friends Holly Wells and Jessica Chapman, aged ten, had attended a barbecue at the Wells' family home. At around 6.15pm they went out to buy some sweets. On their way back, they walked past the house of school caretaker Ian Huntley. Huntley saw the girls and persuaded them to come into his house. He said that his girlfriend, Maxine Carr, their teaching assistant at St Andrew's Primary School, was in the house too. She had, in fact, gone to visit family in Grimsby. Soon after the girls entered his house, Huntley murdered them.

Huntley's motive for killing Wells and Chapman may never be known, although it is assumed that it was sexual. Like Hazell, Huntley is not saying anything. But minutes before luring them into his house, he had reportedly slammed the telephone down on Carr following a furious argument. Apparently, Huntley suspected Carr of cheating on him and he may have killed the girls in a fit of jealous rage.

Soon the search was on. The police released photographs of them wearing Manchester United shirts. Like Hazell, Huntley invited interviews, going on camera with Sky News and the BBC's regional news programme *Look East*. One interviewer suggested to Huntley that he might have been the last person to speak to the girls before they disappeared, to which Huntley replied, 'Yeah, that's what it seems like.'

Adopting the guise of innocence, Huntley said their disappearance was 'absolutely' a mystery and that 'while there's no news, there's still that glimmer of hope, and that's basically what we're all hanging on to'. He, too, played the concerned onlooker.

Maxine Carr also gave interviews, showing a reporter a thank-you card Holly Wells had given her on the last day of the school year. Carr said, 'She was just lovely, really lovely,' and urged the missing girls to 'just come home' – words used by Hazell and Tia's family.

On 16 August, both Huntley and Carr were questioned by the police. After seven hours of questioning they were released. Their home was then searched and they were arrested.

The following day, nearly two weeks after the girls had gone missing, the girls' bodies were found in a ditch near the perimeter fence of RAF Lakenheath in Suffolk, some six miles from Soham. They were severely decomposed and partially skeletonised. Forensic evidence was difficult to obtain from them as Huntley had tried to burn them. Twelve hours later, their clothes were found in the grounds of Soham Village College, where Huntley worked. After attempting to appear insane, Huntley was taken to Belmarsh.

Huntley admitted that the girls had died in his house but, like Hazell, he said it was an accident. He claimed that he had been helping Holly Wells tend a nosebleed when he accidentally knocked her into the bath, where she drowned. Jessica Chapman had witnessed this and he claimed that he had accidentally suffocated her while trying to stifle her screams. By the time he realised what he was doing, it was too late to save either of them. The jury did not accept this and he was found guilty of two counts of murder.

It was then revealed that, like Hazell, Huntley had come to the attention of the police previously. In March 1996 Huntley was charged in connection with a burglary in Grimsby, where he and an accomplice had allegedly stolen electrical goods, jewellery and cash. The case reached court and was ordered to lie on file.

However, unlike Hazell, the other charges against him were of a sexual nature. In August 1995 21-year-old Huntley was investigated by police and social services after a 15-year-old girl said she had been having sex with him. Police did not pursue the case when the girl dropped the charged. In March 1996 Huntley was investigated over allegations of having sex with an underage girl but, again, he was not charged.

A month later Huntley was again investigated over allegations of underage sex but not charged. The month after that it was alleged that he had sex with a 13-year-old girl.

In April 1998 Huntley was arrested on suspicion of raping a woman. He claimed it was consensual. Again, he was not charged. The following month Huntley was charged with the rape of another woman and remanded in custody. The charge was dropped a week later after the Crown Prosecution Service found that there was no chance of a conviction.

In July 1998 Huntley was investigated by the police for allegedly indecently assaulting an 11-year-old girl in September 1997. He was not charged but in April 2007 he admitted attacking the girl. He was investigated over another alleged rape in February 1999 but, again, no charges were laid against him.

Then in July 1999 a woman was raped and Huntley was interviewed as a suspected serial sex offender. This time his girlfriend Maxine Carr gave him an alibi, as she did later in Soham.

At the Old Bailey, Huntley continued with his story that he had killed Holly Wells and Jessica Chapman by accident and pleaded guilty to manslaughter. The jury did not agree and found him guilty on two counts of murder. He was given life. The minimum term was later set at 40 years.

As Maxine Carr had again provided Huntley with an alibi, although she was actually in Grimsby at the time, she was charged with perverting the course of justice and assisting an offender. She pleaded guilty to the first charge and not guilty to the second. The false alibi she provided prompted the police to eliminate Huntley as a suspect in their investigation, delaying his arrest for two weeks.

The court accepted that Carr had lied to the police because she believed that Huntley was innocent and so acquitted her on the charge of assisting an offender. She was sentenced to three-and-a-half years in prison, serving 21 months, including the 16 months she had spent on remand. As threats had been made against her by members of the public, when she was released, she was given a new identity.

Huntley's existence behind bars gives an idea of what Hazell might expect. In 2005 boiling water was thrown over him by another prisoner, quadruple murderer Mark Hobson, and he was badly scalded. The following year he was found unconscious in his cell after attempting suicide by taking an overdose of antidepressants. Then in 2010 he was slashed by fellow prisoner Damien Fowkes. Fowkes pleaded guilty to the attempted murder of Huntley as well as the manslaughter of another child killer, Colin Hatch, who was serving life for the sexually motivated murder of seven-year-old Sean Williams in Finchley, north London, in 1994.

Fowkes told prison officers, 'He's a nonce. He doesn't deserve to live.'

He was serving a life sentence for robbery but his minimum tariff of 5 years, 220 days had already expired by the time he attacked Huntley. Fowkes is now serving life for attempted murder, with a minimum tariff of 20 years.

CHAPTER FOURTEEN

THE AFTERMATH

After the trial, the estate in New Addington struggled to come to terms with what had happened there. Christine Bicknell's house, 20 The Lindens, was sealed up with metal coverings after Tia's body was discovered. Along with the two adjoining houses, it was scheduled to be torn down. But while Hazell was on his way back to prison, more flowers and soft toys were left there as a tribute to the girl he killed.

Eighty-year-old Elizabeth Leigh, who lived just yards away from where the murder took place, said, 'None of us could really believe it when it happened. The step-father had been out searching all week and telling those lies. The community have been very troubled and I think now there will be disappointment we have not got answers.'

She was also distressed that three homes would be destroyed. 'I think it is a waste because it will cost them a lot of money,' she said. 'But they say no one will want to live where the little girl was murdered.'

An elderly neighbour agreed: 'It is inevitable it would happen because it was a child murder. Who would want to move in there now? It is for the best.'

A council spokesman said, 'It is our intention to demolish the properties at 19, 20 and 21 The Lindens, New Addington, as soon as we can following the trial.'

The council feared that they would have difficulty finding new tenants for the properties. The house of next-door neighbour Paul Meehan was also to be bulldozed.

'We then plan to build family homes in their place,' said the Council spokesman. 'There will inevitably be some disruption to neighbours during the demolition and building works but we will aim to keep this to a minimum. We are contacting residents to inform them of these plans.'

Forty-four-year-old Paul Rowland, who lives only metres away from the house where Tia died, said, 'I don't think it will make much difference if they pull them down or just leave them because I don't know if anyone will want to live there anyway.'

But Councillor Simon Hall was worried that the site would receive the sort of interest that followed other prominent murder cases, such as the Gloucester home of serial killers Fred and Rosemary West. 'I don't feel it's right to expect anyone to live in the house or to have it potentially as a place which attracts undue attention over the months or years to come,' he said. 'What we don't want is for people to come and look at the property because "That was the house where Tia was killed", which can sometimes happen in high-profile murder cases. It could really affect people in the area if it was a constant source of attention and would stop them from getting on with their lives.'

Fred and Rosemary West's home at 25 Cromwell Street, where they raped and murdered young women and girls, was demolished and never rebuilt, although the site in New Addington will be redeveloped.

Before the house was due to be knocked down, the family returned to 20 The Lindens one last time. Mark Williams-Thomas was with them. Although it was boarded up, they were allowed to make their way inside. The purpose of the visit? Christine said that she wanted to take Tia away from there with her. Williams-Thomas asked if she had succeeded.

'Not yet,' she said. 'That will be when we close the door for the last time.'

Of the visit, Natalie said, 'I thought it would more… when we walked into it, flooding memories, flashbacks….'

Neighbours looked back on the week between Tia's disappearance and the day the body was found. 'It was the longest time,' said one. 'It seemed so much more than a week. The kids did not get to go outside when it kicked off because it didn't feel safe. It was almost a relief when they arrested him because at least then we knew. And it will be a relief again now as long as he serves a long sentence.'

Also looking back, another neighbour said, 'It was total chaos. We had the police camped out 24 hours a day. We had to sign in and out of our own homes. The police brought us our post and our milk.'

But things have not returned to normal.

'This place is not like it used to be,' said 48-year-old Livina Ofori, who was living in same row of houses as Bicknell and Hazell. 'I have got a young girl who is 16 and her friends used to come round and sleep over all the time. Now they don't want to because they know it as the place Tia Sharp was murdered. I don't know how it will get over it.'

Others are more optimistic.

'The trial has brought back a lot of memories for people,' said Paul Rowland, 'but I think things will go back to normal once everything has calmed down. The community is ready to move on.'

Hazell is not missed by the drinkers of the Randall Tavern. They described him as 'a vile, horrible bully' after he was jailed for a year in 2010 for wielding a weapon after he had been barred. Sixty-five-year-old landlord Peter Wilson, who had run the Randall Tavern for nine years, said, 'He had already been barred from the public house for being aggressive. He came in here with a bunch of flowers and said he was a changed man. I gave him the benefit of the doubt but, after a couple of pints, he was getting aggressive again. I poured his pint into a plastic glass so he could take it with him and asked him to leave. He slammed his beer down on the table so it went all over a man who had been sat there. At that point a couple of customers evicted him. An hour later he came back up to the pub with a machete in his hand.'

Fortunately, the landlord was forewarned. 'We saw him coming up the path carrying a machete,' he said. 'It was about the time the kids were coming out of school. I locked the doors and told everyone to stay inside. Then I called the police.'

Hazell was arrested and convicted of possession of an offensive weapon following the incident and jailed for 12 months. This was one of a number of violent offences he had been convicted for before he murdered Tia.

'He was vile, a horrible bully,' said Wilson. 'He wasn't a regular here but he was not liked around here at all. I did not want him in my pub', he said, adding, 'This estate is full of good people and he made this place look like a slum, which it is not at all.'

Martyn Fox, a regular in the Randall Tavern, said, 'He was a horrible man. He used to come in here bragging about having been in prison.'

Hazell, an accomplished liar, had tried to blame neighbours in the street for Tia's death, pointing the finger particularly at the 'Somalians a few doors down'. According to a neighbour, they did not even exist.

On Tuesday, 14 May, just hours after Hazell had been sentenced, Steven Carter, his partner Melissa Potter, father Steve Carter and other family members quietly visited the estate and the Octagon, the headquarters of the Pathfinders' community group which had helped lead the search for Tia nine months earlier.

Chairman of Pathfinders Marion Burchell said, 'They were overwhelmed with the response the community gave and said, "Thank you all." I cannot believe how dignified they are. Even in their darkest times, they give us strength, as we give them strength. If they had not been such wonderful people and so strong, I don't know how we would have been on the other end. But we are very proud to say that they are friends now.'

Fresh flowers were laid under a tree outside the building

as a tribute to Tia. One bunch bore a card reading, 'Justice has been done.'

The estate had been on tenterhooks waiting for news the morning of Hazell's sentencing. There was relief when they heard that he had got life with a minimum of 38 years.

Eileen Clements, co-owner of the estate's Alwyn Club, which had already planted a small memorial garden and plaque for Tia, said, 'I know it is 38 years but he took a child's life. It is very sad.'

Ward councillor George Ayres said the estate's community had shown great 'compassion, dignity and fortitude' throughout the ordeal. 'I have received, from all over the country, expressions of sympathy and support for Tia's family and the wider community of New Addington,' he said. 'The passing of a child is such a tragic loss that there are no words that can provide the balm to heal the appalling emotional wounds suffered by Tia's family and friends. My heartfelt sympathy goes to each and every one.'

MP Gavin Barwell said, 'The community spirit played a huge role in securing justice for Tia. If the teams had not been scouring the area daily, Hazell may have attempted to move Tia's body, making the job of finding her, and so catching him, all the harder.'

The Patherfinders' Kirsty Pearce added, 'I'd like to say that, at the end of the day, the community did help change the outcome.'

Mr Carter and family also returned to the house where Tia's body had been found. Fresh flowers had been laid there for Tia too in what is said to be another of her favourite colours – yellow. One card said, 'God rest your soul, New Addington's angel.'

Meanwhile, Scotland Yard expressed its concern that Hazell had graduated from being a petty criminal to a murderer. 'It is a massive leap from his previous level of offending to being a child killer,' one Scotland Yard source told *The Times*. 'I'm sure criminologists will be writing papers on this – why did he make that leap? We know he had an interest in child sexual-abuse images, so you have to question the role of the Internet.'

The escalation of Hazell's offending has echoes of the case of Dutch engineer Vincent Tabak, who murdered his neighbour Joanna Yeates in Bristol in December 2010 after becoming fixated with extreme pornographic websites depicting women being strangled. His laptop also contained images of children being sexually abused.

The Child Exploitation and Online Protection Centre (CEOP) warned that the proliferation of child-abuse images and the global growth of high-speed Internet connections had increased the threat to children. John Carr, of the Children's Charities Coalition on Internet Safety, said it was 'unimaginable that the increasing availability of violent and explicit child-abuse imagery can happen without consequences'. Mr Carr advises the Government on Internet regulation and has recommended that web companies should trigger online warnings when attempts are made to access explicit sites. 'It is not easy to generalise,' he said, 'but the offending behaviour of men like Stuart Hazell will be accelerated and amplified by some of the extreme stuff they look for and find online.'

The former head of CEOP, Jim Gamble, said that the Internet could create a 'spiral of abuse'. Having awakened a sexual interest in children, potential offenders meet like-minded individuals. This serves to 'legitimise' their behaviour, he said. 'Ultimately, what they find online is not enough to satisfy them and they can move to attacking a real child in the real world.'

Detectives who questioned Hazell after the killing said his obsession with online pornography 'shaped his behaviour'. It certainly shaped poor Tia's death. Not content with murdering the 12-year-old, he then took photographs of her naked body, posed in the kind of sexual position he saw on these websites.

In 2012 the NSPCC reckoned an average of 35,000 indecent images of children were discovered on the Internet every day. Before the World Wide Web there were just 7,000 such images in circulation at any one time.

The number of people – mostly men – accessing illegal images of children was estimated to have increased by almost 50 per cent in just 4 years. It is thought that the browsers are not just a few weird men on the edge of society; many of them seem to be fairly regular guys whose interest in pornography started 'mildly' then spiralled out of control. Before the Internet they would never have come across this kind of material. And in the real world, they would have been unlikely to meet like-minded people with whom they could discuss and 'normalise' their feelings.

Natalie Sharp spoke out, saying that online access to the billions of child-abuse images should be blocked. She said she wanted Prime Minister David Cameron to put pressure on major Internet firms to stop their search engines being used to access this vile and illegal material, which police fear turned Hazell from petty crook to sadistic monster, happy to kill to fulfil his fantasies. 'David Cameron must force the Internet firms to act swiftly before another child is murdered,' she told the *Sun*. 'As soon as they type in disgusting terms, the Internet companies should block them. How is this sort of thing so readily available?'

Labour MP Diane Abbott warned that online porn is breeding a generation of boys with a twisted, depraved view of women. And the *Sun* called for Internet filth to be blocked at source. 'Images found in the Internet's darkest recesses are fostering a sick "Viagra and Jack Daniels culture",' an editorial said. 'Ministers must respond. We need urgent action to tackle this hidden scandal.'

The NSPCC's Jon Brown said, 'We believe industry, including companies such as Google, could do more to stop people searching for child-abuse images online.'

A spokesperson for the search engine said, 'We take this issue extremely seriously at Google. We are members and joint funders of the Internet Watch Foundation – an independent body that searches the web for child-abuse imagery and then send us links, which we remove from our search index. When we discover child-abuse imagery or are made aware of it, we respond quickly to remove and report it to the appropriate law-enforcement authorities.'

But Hazell's obsession with child pornography came as a surprise to those who knew him. Although Natalie had dated Hazell herself, she said, 'I had no idea he was into child-abuse images. The Stuart we used to know was the last person you would consider to be a paedophile. He was a friend.'

Indeed, she trusted him with her three kids. 'I don't think he came into the family to groom us in order to get access to children,' she said. And she believed that he had never touched Tia sexually before the night he killed her. 'If he had, she would have told me,' Natalie said. 'People said she had more front than Brighton – definitely my daughter.'

In the ITV documentary 'Living with a Killer', she said again that Hazell deserved to suffer for what he had done.

'He doesn't even deserve to be in jail, he doesn't deserve to die,' she said. 'He deserves to suffer. But he'll never suffer, will he? Not like I need him to. He was the last person in my head. I trusted him. I'd known him for ten years. He was supposed to have looked after her.'

She had never suspected a thing, she added. Even after Hazell was convicted, Natalie said, 'It just wasn't in him. As far as I was aware, it wasn't in him. He was gentle. You couldn't have asked for a better person to be around your kids.'

But why hadn't she noticed anything in his behaviour? 'There was nothing to notice. When I was growing up, it was like the bad man was in the dark. The bad man was round the corner. But it's not like that – is it? – no more. The bad man wears a smile. And that smile is a friendly one. And a trusting one.'

Asked, 'He was the last person to see her alive, wasn't he?' She replied in a whisper, 'Yeah, I hate him for that.'

She also talked of the graphic evidence the family had to sit through. 'All he had to do was plead guilty in the first place and no one would have known any of this bad stuff that she had to go through,' she said. 'She could have rested in peace on her own without all of this. And I hate him even more for this.'

Appearing in the same documentary, Christine Bicknell said she thought the schoolgirl was safe being left with her partner but now realises 'she'd have been safer on the streets with a stranger'. She said she had no clue that Hazell was harbouring sick thoughts about her granddaughter. 'He treated me like a queen,' she told the interviewer. 'I lived with a man that I loved with all my heart, that was my world. There's nothing that I should have picked up on. He remained the same as always.'

But looking back after the event, she said, 'It was horrible. I didn't knowingly live with a killer. I knowingly lived with a man I loved with all my heart, who was my world. The thought that he could do that to my own grandchild…'

Merton Council said that the results of the serious case review undertaken in the wake of Tia's death would be published as soon as possible. Serious case reviews are a standard procedure when there has been a suspicious death of a child and abuse or neglect is known or suspected. Its purpose is to examine the role of social services in the case. Until the review was published, the council refused to confirm or deny whether Tia had been on their 'at risk' register.

The independent chair of the MSCB, Kevin Crompton, said, 'Our deepest sympathy goes to Tia's family, friends and the wider community who knew her. The Board is pleased with the outcome of the trial and that justice has been done. Now the trial has ended, we will look to conclude and publish the serious case review as soon as possible.'

Councillor Oonagh Moulton, leader of Merton Conservatives and spokeswoman for education and children's care, said she was pleased justice had been done but that it was important the council was 'held to account', should there have been any failings. 'I am keen to read the report when it becomes available in order to see if further lessons can be learned in order to ensure that our Education, Youth and Children's Services are well managed and that, as far as possible, we can prevent distressing cases such as this from recurring in future,' she said.

With Hazell convicted, forensic psychologist Kerry Daynes reviewed the 40-minute interview he had filmed with ITV News for their documentary, searching for clues. 'During the interview, he is very keen to get across the fact that he feels trapped in his own home,' she said. 'And I am sure he does feel trapped because he's got Tia's body in the attic and she's decomposing and really there are only two choices available to him at that time. He's either got to move Tia from the house or he's got to remove himself from the house.'

As suspicions over what part Hazell played in Tia's disappearance circulated, the family had closed ranks, believing him to be innocent. Tia's uncle David was with Hazell during the interview. He, like the rest of the family, was adamant that Hazell was not involved. During the interview, David had made a public appeal, asking people to stop 'pointing the finger' at Hazell. Afterwards, Hazell had put his arm round him.

'You really see how he values the fact that David is reinforcing that message because David also genuinely feels they are under siege,' said Daynes. 'But David does not realise how desperately Stuart Hazell needs people to take that message on board.'

Christine and the rest of the family had then come under attack and Daynes had a simple explanation for the public reaction: 'There's a tendency to blame really horrific events on the people involved because that allows us to feel reassured. It allows us to maintain the illusion that we are not like these people and, therefore, it cannot happen to us.'

However, she pointed out that this form of scapegoating is not helpful. 'It is very easy to point a finger and say that family should have known. They should have seen the signs that Hazell was interested in Tia in a way that was unhealthy. I am sure the family themselves will be rehearsing that, almost to the point of torturing themselves, thinking, "What was it that I missed?" But the truth is that sexual abuse, by its nature, is very hidden. Nobody advertises the fact that they are sexually interested in children. Stuart Hazell just presented himself as an interested, concerned and loving grandparent, that's all.'

And Daynes' assessment of Hazell?

'It seems that he was having a developing infatuation with Tia. And certainly in the weeks before the murder he was videotaping her sleeping and he was also using an awful lot of pornography, searching for child pornography on the Internet. So it seems that, as Tia was reaching puberty, she was probably becoming more interesting to him. So he planned to assault Tia at some stage. And the opportunity presented itself that evening when she came to stay and Grandma was working.'

Daynes believed the attack was premeditated. This left the family with little consolation.

'It's there. It's a fact. It's happened,' said Natalie. 'It's the hardest thing to come to terms with… to know she is never going to be there again. And that kills me. I'd give anything just to see her once.'

Even Hazell's long prison sentence brought little solace. 'I want him to go to jail for ever. After what he has done, he does not deserve to walk on that pavement. Doesn't even deserve to be in jail, but he doesn't deserve to die. He deserves to suffer.'

To comfort her, Tia's mother has a book of remembrance given to her by Tia's classmates. In it, there is a picture of Tia in her new school uniform. 'I will always remember her smile, her laugh, her voice, the smell of her hair, everything…' said Natalie. 'She'll never leave me.'

The family also have their memories, remembering her for her loud mouth, her 'dodgy dancing' and singing. There are other treasured memories. Tia loved films, music and singing, and would often pretend her BlackBerry was a microphone. On Saturday nights she would be glued to the television for *The X Factor*. Aiming to be an actress herself, she had already given herself star billing. Above her bed her name was spelled out in giant letters on the wall in her favourite pink.

Small for her age, at just 4ft 5in tall, she had a big, infectiously sunny personality. Her happy optimism helped explain why so many cards and flowers were left outside her grandmother's home, where Tia spent much of her time.

'I'll never forget her,' said Christine, 'which means he is always going to be in my life, isn't he? To get rid of him, I have to get rid of her and I can't do that.'

There is another thing that the family will have to live with: the guilt. With Hazell behind bars, public sympathy turned to blame. On 17 May 2013 the *Sun* said, 'How any of her family thought a man, notorious throughout the local community, should be allowed anywhere near a child – never mind left alone – is in itself a crime. These people now have to live with the consequences of their decision, though ultimately the only real victim in all of this is Tia Sharp.'

Steven Carter was singled out for criticism, perhaps unfairly considering that he was a grieving father, by the *Sunday Mirror* when he took centre stage in demanding a death sentence for Tia's killer.

Carter had left Tia's mum Natalie when she was pregnant. 'I did try to keep Tia in her father's life,' she said. 'But when he had a new family, it became obvious to Tia that he didn't want to know.'

'When Tia was murdered,' wrote *Mirror* columnist Carole Malone, 'Carter hadn't seen her for two years, yet when she went missing he was for ever in front of the cameras talking about how he was suffering, how much pain he was in, his life would never be the same…'

She went on to say that maybe Tia wouldn't have become so slavishly devoted to Hazell if she'd had a proper father figure in her life, if her real father hadn't lived miles away with his new family. 'There's no doubt that everyone in this little girl's life let her down… Because Tia Sharp wasn't loved or protected enough by anyone.'

The *People* then claimed that Tia's grandmother Angie Niles had told them that she suspected Hazell four days before her body was found and he was arrested, but had asked them not to print her suspicions, a request that they respected, in case it sparked friction in the family. On 6 August 2012 reporter Aaron Sharp had asked Mrs Niles if there was anyone she thought could have harmed Tia.

'Well, the last person to see her was this Stuart, her grandmother's partner,' she replied. 'Please don't print this, because I don't want to rock the boat and I'm not accusing anyone of anything, but he gives me the creeps. I don't know him and I don't like him. He is saying that Tia left the house at New Addington and got the bus into Croydon but, surely, surely, someone would have seen her. I don't know where she is, I just want her home and I want her safe.'

According to Mrs Niles, the 12-year-old had seemed fearful of going to stay in New Addington. She recalled being brushed off when she asked Tia why she was not staying with Christine Bicknell and Hazell so often. 'She just pulled a face and said, "I'm bored of it, Nangie,"' said Mrs Niles. 'I remember the conversation that we had very vividly. Tia was sat in my front room watching TV. She'd been staying at my house a lot at that time and she hadn't been herself.'

She said she thought that Hazell might have been making advance towards Tia before the fatal attack. 'It's easy to say after the event, but something was wrong and I can't shake the feeling that she wasn't going there for a reason, maybe something had happened,' she told the *People*. 'We've seen what's come out in court, she was still texting him and they were still going to the shops together, but she was a young girl, they're easily swayed. This is a very cunning man; he stayed in the same house as the family for days knowing what he had done.

'Maybe he'd said something, maybe he'd tried it on with her and that's why she didn't want to see him, maybe he'd just been acting strange.'

Again, on the very day Tia's body was found, Mrs Niles had said Hazell was not to be trusted. 'I told everyone,' she said. 'I said on Monday morning, there's something not right about that man. Why is he running from police? I've said it to anyone who will listen. He gave me the creeps. I was shocked, shocked when I opened the papers and read that he had 30 convictions. 30? 3–0?'

She also told the paper that August of the 'emotional time' her family had endured when they were forced to hear graphic details of Hazell's obsession with Tia, including how he took a picture of her naked body after she died. 'It's been a tough time for everybody but in a strange way we also feel relief,' she said. 'He's dragged this out over months insisting he was innocent and only now, at the very last moment, has he put his hands up and admitted what he has done. He deserves to be locked away for ever and have the keys thrown away.'

Meanwhile, Hazell was being guarded 24 hours a day in a special unit for vulnerable criminals, where he was checked on every 15 minutes and guards watched him through a Perspex door. He was kept on a round-the-clock suicide watch and had to be guarded when he exercised, as prison officers feared he would be attacked. While he was being kept in a wing alongside the most despised paedophiles and rapists at the tough jail, he was the prison's most hated inmate and had been sent 'more death threats than Ian Huntley', a source told the *Sunday Mirror* on 19 May 2013.

'Hazell is being kept in a single cell on the most secure wing as he has more death threats than anybody, even more than when Ian Huntley was in the jail,' the paper was told. 'Hazell is in isolation as he is a marked man. He is petrified and shows no inclination to come of out of his cell. He is showing suicidal tendencies. Hazell knows he will have to look over his shoulder every day. He will be shanked [knifed] eventually.'

In his cell in Category A prison Belmarsh in south-east London, he has a bed, a table bolted to the floor and little else. There are no family pictures. From there, he would eventually be moved to Wakefield prison in West Yorkshire. The largest maximum-security prison in Western Europe, it has been dubbed 'Monster Mansion'. Among the other inmates is the legendary Charles Bronson, reputed to be the 'most violent prisoner in Britain'.

'Wakefield has the experience of taking the worst of the worst,' the *Sunday Mirror* reported. 'Hazell is whinging it is miles from London. He thinks it will be too far for people to visit. The reality is, he doesn't get visitors.'

Another letter from prison fell into the hands of the *Sunday Mirror*, who published it. In it, Hazell complained, 'My whole life has been torn apart.' He also moans about not being given counselling and said that he cries himself to sleep.

The letter was littered with spelling errors. He was, he said, living a 'nitemare'. It was written before his dramatic change of plea at a time when he was consumed with self-pity. 'I've never felt so alone in my life,' he wrote. 'I asked the prison for help as some days I get realy down and angry as to what I am accused of and it truly hurts me. I ask for counciling, bereavement counciling as my whole world and everything and everyone who ment the world to me seems to of gone.'

It continues,

Anyway the prison can't help me because I'm a remand prisoner and counciling of any kind is only for sentenced prisoners. What a joke! So basicaly I've been told to deal with it ha ha! And that was off a psychiatrist i've never seen a shrink in my life but when I did it was a waste of time. My whole life has been torn apart and that is what they tell me to do. I know I am inocent and every day is a living nitemare it's like the film *Groundhog Day* I want to wake up and all this is a nitemare.

I feel like I'm stuck in a bubble, it sounds soft but I even cry myself to sleep. Like I said when my cell door closed then I sit and cry, I won't deny it, it truly hurts when people say nasty stuff about me, but if they knew me as me a bloke who would do anything for anyone it would paint a different picture.

He boasted about his gentle nature and said he would never attack a woman.

I've never hit a woman in my life that's a "no no" plus I never even used to tell the kids off, me I used to leave that to other people. I used to get realy badly beaten when I was a kid & I don't even agree in smacking even though some do drive you to it but ive always found it better to sit down a chat. I am a loveing, careing, generous bloke who would do anything for anyone and I would go out of my way to help friends and y-yd. ve he son me in sn't angry & ually im opposite. me wrong if hurt my family I won't just sit there why I have a lot of friends family anyway I could. I will leave prison the same person when I came in and that isn't a bitter, angry & violent actually im the total opposite. Don't get me wrong if somebody hurt my family or friends I won't just sit there and that is why I have a lot of friends out there.

Having little human company, Hazell had befriended a pigeon and compared himself to the 'Birdman of Alcatraz' Robert Stroud, played by Burt Lancaster in the 1962 film of the same name. Convicted killer Stroud raised nearly 300 canaries in the cell at Leavenworth and published 2 books on ornithology. However, when he was transferred to Alcatraz, he was no longer allowed to keep pets. Stroud spent 54 years in prison. Plainly, Hazell was expecting a long stay.

Hazel wrote,

I got a peogion. I think that's how you spell it, but I got one right outside my window and every morning 5 am its Tweet twoo, tweet twoo waiting for me to give it some bread. I feel like the bird man of Alcatraz, I just hope all its mates don't come ha ha. Strange how something so small can take my mind of the cayos [chaos] and madness and this last ten months have been full of cayos and madness believe me. I think my peogion has babies I can hear chirping now but I will do what I do and feed them. Its strange how something so small can cheer me up but like I said I will do what I can to help people even peogions. I'm a big softie & that is what people who know me know what im like.

Hazell also mentioned working in the jail workshop earning – a 's★★t £2 a day... woo hoo' – and his love of sport – 'I watch footie and follow Spurs but I'm more into rugby to be honest.' He supported the Wasps and his favourite TV shows were *Hollyoaks*, *Scrubs*, *How I Met Your Mother* and 'Brits got talent'.

Hazell was plainly a fantasist. He told his family he was 'best mates' with John Altman, who played murderer 'Nasty' Nick Cotton in the BBC soap *EastEnders*. Ruby Tilley, Hazell's 81-year-old grandmother, told the *Daily Mirror* that he boasted about knowing the star. 'He said they were always together,' she said. 'I think he said they met in a pub somewhere.'

'Stuart gave me a picture,' said Mrs Tilley. 'I said, "What's that?" and he said, "A picture of me and my best mate from *EastEnders*."' A spokesman for Altman said the actor had no memory of Hazell, adding, 'He does not know him.' The picture of them together was plainly a posed publicity shot from a chance encounter.

Otherwise, Hazell had been disowned by his family. Mrs Tilley said he deserved to be 'beaten up' by other prisoners. 'If they set about him, he deserves it,' she said. 'He can't go up for parole until he's 75, if he lasts that long. He's got nobody now.'

Even Hazell's father Keith had turned his back on his son after it emerged that he was a paedophile and lusted after Tia, taking a sick photograph of her. Mrs Tilley said that Keith had been in court supporting his son when the picture was shown. 'He didn't think he'd done it,' said Mrs Tilly. I'd never have thought he was a paedophile.'

But that picture convinced Keith Hazell that his son was guilty, Mrs Tilly said. 'Keith said, "When I saw the photo it made me sick. He deserves all he gets. He's no son of mine."'

While sympathy for the family had already turned to anger for their failure to protect her, worse was to come. Word spread that their numerous appearances on TV and interviews with the press had earned them tens of thousands of pounds. The money had started rolling in within weeks of Tia's death.

Apparently, when Tia's relatives went to the TV studios to finish the documentary *Living With A Killer*, they became star-struck, which the *Daily Mail* thought was rather inappropriate. The paper also saw 'some of the extended family [who] were asking for the autographs of the celebrities who work there,' said an onlooker. 'They were very excited to be there.'

According to the *Daily Mail* Tia was just the 'latest victim of the moral decay that now prevails in parts of Britain', the paper said. 'The names may change, they may come from different parts of the country, but all are casualties of the same underclass whose "values" – subsidised in the most part by benefits – are being passed down from generation to generation, from father to son, mother to daughter.'

Looking into the background of Christine Bicknell, the matriarch of the family, the newspaper found that she was the daughter of a warehouse worker and a long-distance lorry driver, Paul Sharp, who had been in and out of prison.

Christine and Paul were married shortly after Natalie was born but the marriage broke up after 18 years. Christine married again in 2004 but her second marriage ended within a few years. At the time, Christine was a barmaid at the Raynes Park Tavern in south-west London.

Around 2002, Christine introduced her own daughter to Stuart, who had already racked up a series of convictions, and they began going out together. Like Christine, Natalie had been a teenage mother, giving birth to Tia when she was 18. Before Tia was born, Natalie had already broken up with Tia's father, Steven Carter, and returned home to New Addington. To her family, Carter was 'just a sperm donor'.

The *Daily Mail* also speculated on why a young woman like Natalie Sharp was attracted to Hazell. Although he was four years her senior, he looked old enough to be her father.

In 2003 Hazell was jailed for nearly three years for selling crack cocaine and heroin. Hazell and the rest of his gang had been caught with wraps of the drugs hidden in their mouths and in their underwear. They were responsible, the police said, for 'misery and crime' in the Kingston-upon-Thames area.

Natalie's relationship with Hazell was short-lived. It lasted only a matter of weeks and appears to have been over before he was convicted.

The papers have had their say but none of this detracts from the tragedy of Tia Sharp, a young girl whose life was snuffed out before it had hardly begun. Long after the trial, outside the house in New Addington, someone had left a fresh bouquet with poem attached to it. It began,

> Three little words
> Forget me not
> They don't say much but mean a lot
> Forget you not, we never will

EPILOGUE

Stuart Hazell changed his plea, so we never got to hear the case for the defence. However, Mark Bridger, while admitting that he was responsible for the death of April Jones, continued with his plea of not guilty to abduction, murder and perverting the course of justice. His defence began a week after Hazell was sentenced and his cross-examination at the trial gives a useful insight into the mind of the paedophile murderer, fuelled by alcohol and drugs, which both he and Hazell proved to be. Bridger's case is worth a brief study, seeing as the two cases share so many similarities.

In her opening statement, the prosecutor Elwen Evans QC had said, 'It's our case that the defendant's actions – abduction, murder, covering up what he has done – that his actions were sexually motivated. He has played, we say, a cruel game in pretending not to know what he has done to her. It's a game to try and save himself and try to manipulate his way out of his full responsibility in what he has done.'

She began her cross-examination by asking, 'Where is April?'

Bridger replied, 'I don't know, I really don't know.'

He was then asked to look at the image he viewed at 12.11pm 'on the day April was abducted by you'. Bridger took exception to being accused of abducting April, so the prosecution agreed to use the neutral phrase of 'the day she left Bryn-y-Gog in your car'.

Bridger was then probed about his 'fantasy' career in the army. He agreed that stories of how he had trained in places like Namibia, Afghanistan and Cuba were all lies. But he said that his lies 'could not have been good' as no one seemed to believe him.

He was then cross-questioned about lies he had told the police. 'You have to remember I am an alcoholic who hadn't had a drink for a number of days,' he said.

The prosecution then asked him again whether he got any sexual gratification from the pornographic images found on his computer. Again, he said that he did not.

Bridger then claimed that his talk of being in the army was a fabrication, rather than a lie. 'A fabrication was something to make up to impress someone, rather than to deceive,' he said. 'Fantasy is what you wish to have happened. A lie is that you are adamant that what you a saying is different to what happened.'

He then maintained that April's seven-year-old friend, who'd said the five-year-old was 'happy and smiling' when she climbed into his Land Rover, was lying: 'I believe she has lied about what she saw and that she's confused about other things, such as the colour and description of the car. This is a seven-year-old child who is frightened. She's just lost her friend, she's seen her friend disappear.'

Bridger was then challenged that his recollection of the alleged road accident was 'incredibly detailed' for someone who claimed to have poor recollection about the events that immediately followed it. He replied that his recollection of the accident was only 'reasonably detailed'.

The prosecution then referred him to the evidence he had given about his attempts to resuscitate April. However, he was seen only six minutes after he had parked up on the Bryn-y-Gog estate driving passed the Tuffins garage some way away.

Bridger insisted that he had tried to save April, but he could not remember half the journey, although he did concede, 'That little girl died that night due to me.'

Elwen Evans then asked, 'When was it that this fog of not knowing descended on you?' Bridger said that he remembered nothing after that. 'I felt numb, I felt sick, I was frightened and in fear. This little girl was dead in my car, you can't tell me you know how that feels,' he said.

However, when he was seen with a black bin bag in a lay-by the following morning, Bridger said he was retrieving it after it had blown out of his car. 'It was a wet and windy day,' he said.

Ms Evans then put it to Bridger that he could have done 'anything' to April because he could not remember. But he was insistent: 'I couldn't have done anything. There's no DNA evidence on myself or on my person that I had sexual contact with her. There's no evidence of sexual contact in my car. There's no evidence I had sexual contact in my house. There's no evidential evidence that I struck April.'

'Do you accept that you killed April?' Ms Evans asked.

'I did not kill her, I caused her death,' he replied. 'To me, to kill means you go out and deliberately do that, I didn't do that. I did cause the death of April and I have never denied that.'

He was then asked how he 'disposed' of April's body. '"Dispose" is such a horrible way of putting it,' Bridger said. 'Her body has not been found.'

Again, he did not recall cleaning up his house. 'You have suggested this is a huge clean-up,' Bridger said. 'What I'm saying is, if I saw blood on the floor, I would have wiped it up. I'm a single man who lives on my own. The areas I used most I cleaned every single day. I did not live a in a pigsty.'

He admitted looking at child pornography the day April went missing. 'I clicked on an image of child pornography, yes,' he said.

Bridger had already told the court that he changed his facial appearance every month. The day April went missing, he shaved off his beard and cut his hair. He said he 'believed' he did this because there was a parents' evening at his daughter's school and he wanted to make a good impression on her teachers.

He also told a custody officer at Aberystwyth Police Station that he did not think he would have put April's body in a river. 'Although I was a lifeguard, I do have a fear of drowning myself,' Bridger said.

So why had he lied to people on 2 October, saying he had not heard about April's disappearance until that morning? 'What was I supposed to do?' he said. 'Turn around and say yes, I had killed the girl last night? I wasn't telling lies. I just didn't tell the whole truth. I was still trying to come to terms that this little girl had died because of me. I was still coming to terms with where I had put her.'

The knives and axes found in his house were used to chop wood for the log burner and make handles for other knives and axes, he said. The burned boning knife found on top of his log burner had been put there months before. It had a broken plastic handle, which he was trying to melt off, before giving it a new one.

Two pairs of handcuffs were also found in his home. He kept them for 'decoration purposes', he said. 'They've never been used for any sexual purpose,' he said.

While he was in prison, he said he recalled lying April down in front of the wood stove. Asked why he had done that, he said, 'I can only speculate. She was dead by that time and, in some silly way, by placing her in front of the fire, it would have been peace and quiet for her, warm for her... I didn't lay her on the sofa or on the chair.'

However, he had no recollection of cleaning or wiping up the carpet. But why had he lit the stove on the morning of 2 October? A police helicopter had photographed the smoke. He said he had 'no idea'.

'Why in the middle of all of the panic, distress and dismay would you light a fire?' Ms Evans asked. 'It's an automatic thing if it's cold... it might have been cold,' he said. 'I don't know, it's something that's done.' He said he cooked chicken, pork and beef on the coals. Remains of a number of animals had been found, including the full skeleton of a rabbit and a squirrel.

Bridger claimed that forensic experts had missed vital evidence of the accident when they examined his Land Rover. No traces of blood had been found in it. They had also failed to examine the place where he claimed to have knocked April down, he said.

When Bridger denied being a paedophile, he was asked, 'Why do you have images of children?' He replied, 'Lots of them were looking into the development of my two youngest children.'

The prosecution put it to him that this was 'complete fantasy'. Bridger also claimed that he had named a file on his laptop after a local girl because his children had asked him to.

It then transpired that Bridger had hidden his age on his Facebook account. Then he was asked why, at the age of 45, he had invited one of April's teenage half-sisters to be his friend. 'Because I've known her for two and a half years. I knew her family,' he said. However, he accepted that she may only have known him by sight. 'I didn't think it was inappropriate,' he said.

So why were pictures of April's half-sisters in a folder that also contained child pornography? 'They shouldn't have been there,' Bridger admitted.

Another picture saved in the folder was of a young girl wearing a T-shirt with the words 'work in progress' across her breasts with an arrow pointing to her private parts, followed by the words 'good to go'. Bridger said he had never seen this picture before.

There was also an indecent image of young girl on a beach and a close-up of a sex act on his laptop. Bridger explained that the picture of the girl on the beach was 'perfect' to show his daughter to help her understand her own development, while the close up of the sex act would be part of his children's sex education. 'I'd be quite happy showing my son and daughter this as the first stage of learning sexual stuff,' he said.

He had also viewed a picture of a 6-year-old local girl on 28 and 30 September. He said he might have noticed that it was her birthday.

Along with pictures of local girls and child pornography, he also had pictures from naturist sites. One showed a naked young girl standing next to a naked woman, both with a snake around their necks. This was a 'beautiful example' of a picture of a young girl 'going through changes,' he said.

Another picture showed a young girl who Bridger now claimed might have been his daughter. But had he not even 'hinted' at that during his police interviews? 'Because I didn't expect to be charged with abduction or murder,' he responded.

A picture of a young girl in school uniform was also in the folder of child pornography. He said that a former partner had downloaded it from a catalogue. He did not know how it got into that folder because he was not 'a computer expert'.

Bridger told the jury that he had written letters of complaint to the companies that put these indecent images on the Internet. He had written their addresses down on scraps of paper, then fired off a hand-written letter of complaint. After that, he would burn the addresses or throw them away.

Bridger was then why he asked a ten-year-old girl if she

wanted a sleepover with his daughter hours before April was allegedly abducted. 'Do you think it is appropriate that you, a single man, with a broken relationship, in drink, to invite a young girl for a sleepover?' Ms Evans asked. I wasn't making advances, I wasn't asking her to sleep with me,' Bridger replied. 'I was asking her to have a sleepover with my daughter.' He added he did not think there was anything 'cynical' about the invitation.

Originally, Bridger had told police he had not spoken to the ten-year-old girl about coming over to his house for a sleepover. He now conceded he had. He told the court that, at the time, he didn't think he had spoken to her at all. 'I didn't know I had. I thought I had waved at her.'

Ms Evans then asked Bridger what he was doing when he was spotted on the Bryn-y-Gog estate slouched in his car with a newspaper on his lap, talking into a walkie-talkie. Bridger said the witness who claimed to have seen him was mistaken. 'I've never bought a newspaper, I don't read newspapers,' he said.

He was then asked to describe his state of mind on the morning of 2 October, the morning after April went missing. 'I'm in a completely different state to normal,' he said. 'I would've still had my drinks but the realisation of killing a child is with me as well. I'm distressed, I'm upset, I've had a drink, I've got to find out what happened. It's slightly different to a normal morning.'

Ms Evans then asked him whether he had spared a thought for April's parents on the morning of 2 October and whether he was aware of the search that was going on.

'I cannot even start to understand what they were going through but, at the time, I didn't know April had not been

258

found,' he said. 'It was only speaking to Cheryl [his employer] and the postman [that] I realised there was a huge search going on for her.'

After discovering the person he had killed was April, he decided to take his Land Rover to the garage. Why had he done that? 'I had problems with my car,' he said. 'It was on the way to the police station.'

But Bridger did not go to the police station. He did not report the alleged accident. Instead, he decided to go back to Ceinws and look for April, he said.

The jury was then shown the footage of Bridger out walking that morning, taken by a police helicopter. Ms Evans asked Bridger whether he agreed the recording showed a man who was calm out walking his dog, not a man who was distressed or panicking.

Bridger said that the footage from the helicopter did not show whether he was crying. 'I had my stick, I had my torch around my neck, the dog with me,' he said. 'I was out looking, trying to remember.'

Bridger accused Ms Evans of 'twisting' his answers. 'I have to be very careful about what I say to you because you twist things to make it sound like I'm lying,' he said.

Bridger was then asked whether the 'alarm bells were ringing' when he received a text message from a former partner telling him that police were looking for a van or a Land Rover. 'No,' he said.

Ms Evans accused Bridger of lying about driving repeatedly around Machynlleth after allegedly knocking April down. 'That's what I believed I did,' he said.

So had he 'abandoned' that story when he learned CCTV proved he had driven directly out of the town?

'No, I've never abandoned that,' he said. 'I still believe I drove around a number of times.'

Bridger was then confronted with his Defence Case Statement – a document drawn up before trial that provides an outline of his defence. There were a number of discrepancies between this and the evidence he gave in court, Ms Evans said.

He then said he was not involved in a 'collision' involving April on the Bryn-y-Gog estate. Rather, he said he must have run over her after she had already fallen off her bicycle or when she had leaned down to pick something up.

The jury were told that, in his statement, Bridger had not mentioned anything about the 'crusade' against pornography companies that he now claimed to be waging. Nor did he mention that the images could have been downloaded by his former partner. There was also no mention of the black bin bag or the beige fleece he claimed to have rinsed in his bath. Ms Evans then suggested that Bridger's version of the events of the night of 1 October and 2 October were 'a fantasy, a fabrication and a lie'. He denied this.

'Your actions that night were clearly dedicated actions,' Ms Evans said.

'No,' Bridger replied.

'Whether you were drunk or not, you knew what you were doing,' she added.

'No,' he said again.

'You abducted April.'

'No, I had no reason to abduct April.'

'What did you say to get her into your car?'

'I never spoke to her,' he said.

'You have a sexual interest in children,' Ms Evans continued.

'No,' he said.

'Having murdered her, you disposed of her body,' Ms Evans said.

'I placed her body somewhere,' Bridger replied.

Again the prosecutor asked, 'What did you do with April?'

'I crushed her with my car,' said Bridger

'What did you do with April's body?'

'I don't know, I don't know,' he said.

Ms Evans then asked him to take a minute to focus on where he put April's body.

'I have done for the last nine months,' said Bridger.

'And what answers have you come up with?' she said.

'I don't have any answers, I'm sorry,' he replied.

That was the end of the cross-examination and the end of the case for the defence, barring the closing statement. To the end, Bridger refused to tell April's grieving parents where the body of their daughter lies. Perhaps, like Moors murderer Ian Brady, he feels that withholding that vital piece of information still gives him a modicum of control.

After the closing statements and the judge's summing up, the jury was out for four hours and six minutes, and returned a verdict of guilty on all counts. Bridger will serve the rest of his life in jail. Although Hazell was given a minimum tariff of 38 years, he is unlikely to be let out either. Like Ian Huntley, they will suffer at the hands of other prisoners. And I can't say that I am sorry.